THE
PRACTICAL TELEPHONE HANDBOOK.

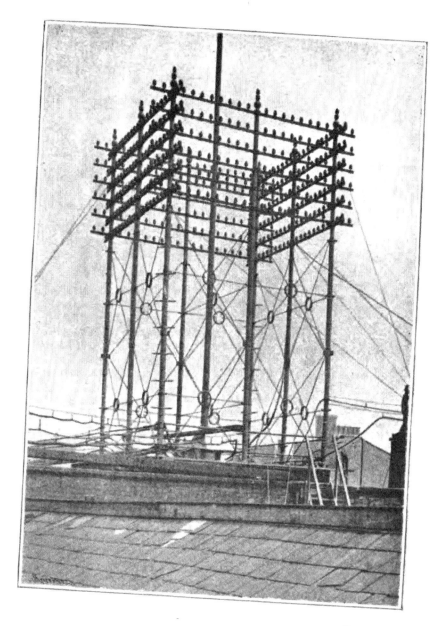

Frontispiece.

THE

PRACTICAL
TELEPHONE HANDBOOK

AND

GUIDE TO THE TELEPHONIC EXCHANGE.

BY

JOSEPH POOLE, *Whitworth Scholar* (1875),

CHIEF ELECTRICIAN TO THE LATE LANCASHIRE AND CHESHIRE
TELEPHONIC EXCHANGE CO., MANCHESTER.

WITH 227 ILLUSTRATIONS.

LONDON:
WHITTAKER & CO., 2, WHITE HART STREET,
PATERNOSTER SQUARE, E.C.
GEORGE BELL & SONS, YORK STREET, COVENT GARDEN.

1891.

PREFACE.

In the following book the writer has endeavoured to produce a manual of moderate size and cost, but thoroughly practical, and detailing, as far as space would allow, the most recent methods of telephonic working.

Whilst the requirements of telephone *employés* have been constantly kept in view, it is fully intended, also, that the book shall be of service as a source of information on telephonic matters to users of the telephone and to the public generally.

The text is supplemented by a large number of illustrations, mostly drawn to scale by the writer, and, wherever desirable, diagrams of the electrical connections of the instruments described have been given.

The writer's long experience has proved to him the very injurious action of electro-magnets included directly in telephonic circuits, owing to their electro-magnetic inertia, and he has made a point of indicating how this evil may be got rid of or minimized.

The writer's thanks are due to those firms who have kindly lent blocks for illustration, and to other friends who have assisted him with drawings, etc., especially to Mr. A. R. Bennett, to whom the progress of telephony is much indebted. The abstract of a paper by Mr. Bennett, which is given at the end, would, it was thought, fitly close the book, as dealing with what is likely to be the future of the telephone.

For the photograph from which Fig. 150 was produced, the writer is indebted to Mr. J. W. Wade.

Special thanks are due from the writer to his friend Mr. J. H. Shorrocks, to whom he is very much indebted for the great assistance rendered in the preparation and revision of the book.

CONTENTS.

CONTENTS.

LIST OF ILLUSTRATIONS.

PRACTICAL TELEPHONE HANDBOOK.

———•◦•———

CHAPTER I.

PRELIMINARY.

BEFORE proceeding to the subject proper, it will be advisable to define the various terms used by telephonists, so that no misunderstanding may afterwards arise as to their correct meaning.

Electric Current.—When electricity is in motion, or is propagated from one point to another, certain effects are produced upon adjacent bodies.   These effects—magnetism, motion, heat, chemical changes, etc.—are said to be due to an *electric current.*

As *electric* currents are the only currents that will be dealt with in this book, no misunderstanding should arise if the term *electric* is dropped.

Strength of a Current.—This is measured by the intensity of the effects produced.

Resistance.—An infinite variety of strengths of current may be obtained by including different substances and different masses of these substances in the path of a current. The cause of the various strengths is due to the different *resistances* which these materials oppose to electricity in motion.

All bodies offer some resistance, which is found to be in direct proportion to the length-of any material of uniform section and quality, and inversely proportional to the area of section or to the square of its diameter. Resistance also varies with the temperature of the material, that of metallic bodies increasing with a rise of temperature, and that of non-metallic bodies decreasing, of some, such as carbon, very markedly.

Conductivity.—Substances, such as the metals, which offer the least resistance are called good conductors, or are said to have a *good conductivity*. This term is therefore the converse of resistance.

Of the metals, pure silver and copper offer the least resistance. If that offered by a piece of pure silver is taken as the unit, the resistance of the more common metals and other substances will be approximately as follows :—

Pure Silver   1

,,   Copper   1·04

,,   Platinum 5·74

,,   Iron   6·04

,,   Lead   12·8

,,   Mercury 59

,,   Carbon 1,450 to 40,000

Liquids, Dilute Sulphuric Acid ($\frac{1}{15}$ acid)   2,062,000
       Pure Water   44,000,000
       Glass   14,000,000,000,000
       Gutta-percha 210,000,000,000,000,000,000,000

Insulators.—From this list it will be seen that glass and gutta-percha offer an immense resistance to the passage of the current, therefore these, and substances such as porcelain, india-rubber, and ebonite, are selected to confine the current to a certain path by acting as supports to the conducting materials. They are therefore called insulators, and are of great importance in practical electrical matters.

Potential.—The strength of the current which can pass through a path of a certain resistance depends upon the difference between two points of that path, in regard to what is called the *potential* of the electricity. This is a property of electricity analogous to the pressure of steam or level of water in regard to their power of doing work. The greater the difference in level of two reservoirs of water, the stronger will be the flow of the water through a certain sized pipe from one to the other, and the more work could be done by this flow. So with electrical currents, the greater the *difference of potential* between any two points of a conducting path, the stronger will be the current along that path. Potential is sometimes called *electrical pressure*.

Electro-motive Force.—Any arrangement which can produce a difference of potential is said to have an *electro-motive force*, which term is usually abbreviated to E.M.F. There are many methods of causing a difference of potential, such as by means of voltaic batteries, magneto-electric machines, and dynamo machines.

Volt.—Difference of potential, or E.M.F., is compared by reference to a practical unit called the *volt*, a little less than the E.M.F. of a Daniell cell, which is 1·065 volts.

The Leclanché cell has an E.M.F. of 1·46 volts.

The Ohm is the unit in which all measurements of resistance are expressed. It is the resistance of a column of mercury 106·25 centimetres long, and one square millimetre in section at a temperature of 0° centigrade.

A better idea of this resistance will be obtained by giving the length of some common materials offering 1 ohm resistance, such as—

2·48 feet of copper wire $\frac{1}{100}$-inch in diameter. This is the size of wire used for winding most telephone receiver bobbins.

430 feet or 143 yards of copper wire $\frac{1}{16}$-inch diameter, which is the wire used for the lines of telephone exchange subcribers.

71 feet of iron wire $\frac{1}{16}$ inch diameter.

Very high resistances are measured in *Megohms*. One megohm = one million ohms.

Ampère.—The unit strength of current is called the ampère, and is such a current as would be sent through a resistance of 1 ohm by an E.M.F. of 1 volt.

The *Milliampère*, equal to the $\frac{1}{1000}$th part of an ampère, is often used as a unit in telephony.

The Circuit.—The whole path through which a generator of electricity sends a current is called a *circuit.* It always forms a closed loop. When a current is passing the circuit is said to be *closed*, or *complete.* When the continuity of the conductors is broken by interposing an insulating body, the current ceases, and the circuit is said to be *open*, or *broken.* Some current, however, passes through substances of the highest resistance, so that the above only applies to the *useful* current.

Earth.—The circuit may be made up of different substances. In most cases it is made up of wires, but even bad conductors, such as earth or water, may form part of a useful circuit when in large masses. For economy, the earth is often used to complete a circuit for a telephone connection, in order to save a second wire between the places connected. In making such a connection it is of the utmost importance that a conductor having a large surface in contact with the earth or water should be used as a medium of connection between the wire and the earth. For this purpose the water pipes of a town's water supply are always chosen. If they are not available, large iron or copper plates are buried in damp ground, and the circuit wires connected to them.

By a *metallic circuit* is meant one of which the earth does not form a part, being made wholly of metal. Metallic circuits are becoming more extensively employed, because the use of the earth for telephonic working brings many disadvantages with it.

If in an ordinary circuit different conductors follow one after the other, these conductors are said to be joined up in *series*.

The resistance of a circuit is the sum of the resistances of its different parts joined up in series, and includes the resistance of the generator itself, called its *internal* resistance. A circuit may be divided into several branches, which must all come together again at some point. These branches are called *derived, divided, branch,* or *shunt* circuits. A current flows through a divided circuit in proportion to the conductivity, or inversely proportional to the resistance of each branch.

Resistance of Divided Circuits.—If each branch of a divided circuit is equal, the combined resistance of them all will be equal to that of one branch divided by the number of branches. If they are unequal, their combined resistance will be equal to *the reciprocal of the sum of the reciprocals of the resistances* of the several branches. The reciprocal of a number is unity, or one, divided by that number. The reciprocal of $20 = \frac{1}{20}$ or ·05, that of $30 = \frac{1}{30}$ or ·033, and the reciprocals of ·05 and ·033 = 20 and 30 respectively. Suppose a divided circuit made up of two wires whose resistance are 20 and 30 ohms. The combined resistance of the two wires would be equal to the reciprocal of $\frac{1}{20} + \frac{1}{30}$. $\frac{1}{20} + \frac{1}{30} = \frac{20+30}{20\times30}$ and the reciprocal of this $= \frac{20\times30}{20+30} = 12$; or, working by decimals, ·05 + ·033 = ·083, the reciprocal of which = 12 as before.

Short Circuit.—A derived circuit of very low resistance compared to the resistance of the other branch or branches, is called a *short circuit.* It robs the other circuits of nearly all current.

Ohm's Law.—This law is the most important one in electrical matters, and states :—That if the resistance of a circuit be expressed in ohms and the total E.M.F. in volts, then the strength of the current produced will be given in ampères by dividing the latter by the former. If R represents resistance in ohms, E the volts, and C ampères, the relation between the three will be expressed by $C = \frac{E}{R}$ or E=CR or $R = \frac{E}{C}$ so that, given any two of these quantities, the third may be easily obtained.

Ohm's law applies to any portion of a circuit, as well as to a whole circuit.

MAGNETISM.—*Magnetic Lines of Force.*—The reader will be familiar with the beautiful curves in which iron filings sprinkled over a card covering a magnet set themselves, as shown in Fig. 1. At the poles or strongest points the lines are clustered together, and spread out from these points in symmetrical curves. These curves are only sections of the *magnetic field* surrounding the magnet, and show the direction in which the magnetic action extends, and in which small magnetic needles free to move would set themselves. A piece of soft iron in the neighbourhood of the magnet modifies the magnetic field, and the curves are altered in shape, appearing to be attracted to the iron, so that a greater number of the lines pass through the space occupied by the iron than there did formerly. In passing through the iron the lines of force convert it into a magnet.

These lines of force have become of the greatest consequence to electricians, and the idea of them is much employed in magnetic measurements. The intensity of magnetism at any part is proportional to the number of lines of force which pass through a certain unit space.

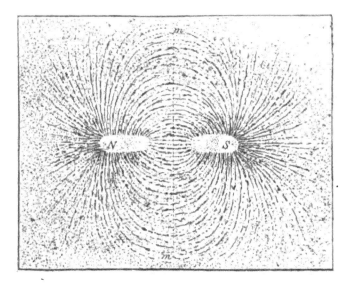

Fig. 1.

Magnets. — The simplest form of magnet is the straight *bar magnet.* *Horse-shoe* ones are, however, much stronger, the poles being close together and the lines of force clustered together between them. They have about three or four times the attractive power on a piece of soft iron near their poles that a bar magnet of the same size would exert.

Thin bars or plates of steel can be more powerfully magnetised in proportion to their weight, therefore when a strong permanent magnet is required it is generally made up of several thin plates, producing what is called a *compound* or *laminated* magnet. The plates are usually bound together by pieces of soft iron, which form the pole-pieces. Some compound magnets have been made which would carry a load equal to 25 times their own weight. The best cast steel, with an addition of 3 per cent. of *tungsten*, makes the best magnet steel, the value of which depends upon what is called its *coercive* force, or its resistance to change in its magnetic state. This coercive force is the greater the harder the steel is tempered. By a process, however, of subjecting the steel to very great pressure, M. Clemandot has given a high coercive force to it, with the advantage that the metal can be filed, turned, etc., without impairing its magnetic value.

Magnetising.—The best method of magnetising is by means of a strong electro-magnet furnished with a large pole-piece. The steel is drawn over the pole, always in the same direction, some 20 or 30 times.

Small magnets, such as the needles of galvanometers, are liable to lose their magnetism from various causes, such as lightning discharges or strong currents. For such purposes it is much better to use a soft iron needle polarized by means of comparatively large magnets fixed near.

Currents Induced by Magnets.—Faraday's discovery that electric currents could be caused to flow through a coil of wire by the approach or recession of a magnet is of the greatest service in telephony, Bell's original telephone being based upon it. These induced currents are only momentary ones, lasting as long as the movement. They are in strength proportional to the strength of the magnet, the speed of its movement, and the number of turns of wire in the coil. The direction of the currents is dependent on which pole of the magnet is used, one producing opposite currents to the other. Also the currents produced by approach are opposite in direction to those produced by recession of the same pole.

Relative motion is all that is necessary, so that the same effects are produced by moving the coil to or from the magnet.

Faraday showed that to produce the currents it was necessary that the number of lines of force passing through the coil should vary with the movement, and that the strength of the induced currents was proportional to this variation.

Lenz's Law is applicable to all electrical induced effects, and states :—That " the induced currents have such a direction that their reaction tends to stop the motion or current which produces them."

Current Induction.—Wires conveying electric currents also exhibit magnetic properties, and are surrounded with a magnetic field and lines of force. A section of this field may be shown by passing a wire conveying a strong current vertically through a horizontal card and sprinkling iron filings over the card, the filings will arrange themselves in concentric circles round the wire, as in Fig. 2, which gives a plan of the card and section of the wire. Each filing is really made into a magnet by the lines of force passing through it, and a small freely suspended magnetic needle would set itself as a tangent to one of the circles.

When the wire is bent into a circle, a large number of these lines of force come together in the interior, and the magnetic action there is consequently more intense than in the case of a straight wire, and is still further increased when the wire makes a number of turns and forms a coil.

The Electro-magnet is constructed on this principle, the lines of force passing through the soft iron core inside the coil or coils, rendering it powerfully magnetic.

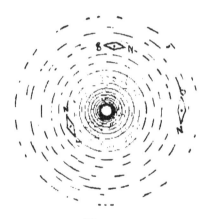

Fig. 2.

The practical points in connection with electromagnets are as follows :—The cores, armature, and other ironwork should be made of the softest iron, well annealed, and should not afterwards be turned or filed, so that it may be rendered strongly magnetic by the current, or, in other words, have a high degree of *permeability*, and may lose as much as possible of its magnetism on the current ceasing. To attain the latter object it [is necessary that the armature be prevented from coming into actual contact with the iron of the cores, which would allow the *magnetic* circuit to be completed if a horse-shoe magnet, and would give rise to the *sticking* of the armature, due to the residual magnetism which would exist after the current ceased. To prevent this sticking it is usual to drill small holes in the ends of the cores, in which are inserted *core pins* of brass wire, projecting very slightly past the ends of the core.

The number of turns of wire on the coils should be large when the magnet has to form part of a circuit of high resistance. This entails the use of thin wire for winding. When for a circuit of low resistance it is best to use thick wire, but the number of turns should be as large as the bobbin will allow.

The wire in the coils (if there are two) must be connected up in such a manner that the windings would be continuous in one direction if the magnet were straightened out.

In the *Galvanometer* a small magnetic needle takes the place of the core of the electro-magnet. It is so pivoted inside the coil that by gravity, or the earth's magnetic action, it tends to set itself in a line with the direction of the wire forming the coils. When a current passes through the coils, its magnetic action tends to set the needle at right angles or along the axis of the coil.

The galvanometer mostly used in telephonic work for testing batteries, tracing faults, etc., is shown in Fig. 3,

and is called a lineman's *detector*. The magnetic needle
is inside, that outside being merely a pointer attached to
the same pivot.   It is generally furnished with two coils
of wire : one, consisting of a few turns of thick wire,
used for roughly measuring low resistances, such as the
internal resistance of a battery; the other coil is made
up óf a large number of turns of thin wire, having a
resistance of 100 or 200 ohms.   The latter coil is used

for testing circuits of a high resistance, and for roughly measuring the E.M.F. of batteries.

The Induction Coil is made by
winding over an electro-magnet
coil another coil, usually of fine
wire, with a large number of
turns.   Whenever the current
in the *electro-magnet* or *primary*
coil of wire is started or stopped,
or its strength varied, induced
currents are produced in the

Fig. 3.

other or *secondary* coil if the circuit of the latter is
complete.   The starting or strengthening of a current
has thè same effect as bringing up a magnet to the
coil, and the stopping or weakening, the same effect
as taking away the magnet from the coil.   The
strengths of the induced currents depend upon the
number of turns of wire on both coils, and the rate of
variation in the strength of the magnetising or primary
current.   The cores of induction coils are usually made
up of a bundle of thin iron wires, in order to reduce the

reactive effect on the primary current, and because it has been found that such cores gain and lose magnetism more quickly than solid ones, and a greater rate of variation in the magnetism can therefore be obtained.

Induction of Straight Wires.—Owing to its magnetic action, a current passing through a straight wire will induce currents in another wire running parallel, when the current is varied in strength. The current induced on starting or strengthening the primary one is in the opposite direction, that on stopping or weakening in the same direction. The reaction of the induced currents weakens and opposes the primary ones, according to Lenz's law. The strength of the induced currents depends upon the rate of variation of the primary current, the distance apart of the wires, the lengths they run together, and the insulating substance or *dielectric* between them.

The induction through dry air is less than when any other substance intervenes between the wires. What is called the *inductive capacity* of air being unity, that of resin=1·7, glass 1·9, paraffin 1·98, india-rubber 2·8, and gutta-percha 4·2.

It is important to consider these values in connection with cables for telephone wires, and, if otherwise possible, to choose a substance which has the least inductive capacity, and so keep down the inducing action between the wires.

Self-Induction.—Any wire conveying a current may be looked upon as made up of a multitude of small wires connected together, each conveying a portion of the current. Each of these small currents reacts momentarily on the others whenever its strength is varied, tending to oppose them. This is called the *self-induction* of a current, and its power depends upon the shape of the conductor. Anything which tends to separate the contiguous portions, such as flattening the wire or *stranding* the conductor—that is, making it up of several small wires—reduces the self-induction.

Electro-magnetic Inertia.—The magnetic property of iron wires has a harmful influence on currents rapidly varying in strength which pass through them. Such are the currents which pass through the telephone wires in conveying speech. A part of the energy of such currents is wasted in magnetising the material of the wire. The weakening is said to be due to the *electro-magnetic inertia* of the wire.

Both self-induction and electro-magnetic inertia are met with in a high degree in connection with electro-magnets. Each turn of the coil acts on the other turns as though it were an independent circuit, and thereby produces intense self-induction, which is much increased by the magnetisation of the core. The magnetising of the core also robs the current of much of its energy when it rapidly varies in strength.

In consequence of the above action of electro-magnets much attention has lately been drawn to the injurious effects of introducing them into a telephone circuit. Their action is said to be due to an *impedance* in the path of the currents, which weakens the transmitted speech ·ery materially. The more iron there is in connecti·n with the electro-magnets, the more marked is the e· ·. Making up the cores of soft iron wires reduces · some extent the impedance of the electro-magnets.

Static Induction.— The inducing effects hitherto mentioned have been due to dynamical or magnetic action, but somewhat similar results are produced by the *stati·* *l* electric action of one conductor on another. This actu·n has considerable importance in telephonic matters. Every current passing through a wire charges it with static or frictional electricity, the charge depending upon the potential of the current, the surface of the conductor charged, the proximity of other conductors, and the specific inductive capacity of the substances intervening between the conductors. This charging weaker the original current, especially when very rapid·· riations of potential are concerned, its effect being especially marked in cables where the conductors are close together. It is principally this which prevents telephonic speaking through any long length of submarine cable. On overhead land lines its effect is comparatively small, as the conductors are wide apart and are separated by air, which has the least inductive capacity. It seems very likely, however, that much of the overhearing on land lines is due to static induction.

Microfarad.—The unit of capacity is the *Farad*, but the practical unit is the one-millionth part of this, called the *microfarad*. About three miles of submarine cable will have one microfarad capacity.

Wire Gauges.—Wires were formerly compared in size by the Birmingham wire gauge, but its unreliability—from the fact that several different gauges existed, all professing to be the B. W. G.—led to the British Board of Trade issuing what is called the *British Imperial Standard Wire Gauge,* a list of some of the sizes of which, compared with the most reliable B. W. G., is given at the end of the book.

The Mil.—A better way of comparing wires is to give their diameter in thousandths of an inch, which are called *mils.*
This mil must not be confounded with the French millimetre, which is equal to about 40 mils. A micrometer gauge is necessary to measure in mils, and a very convenient one

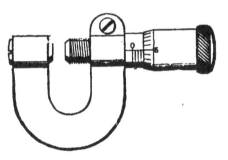

Fig. 4.

for the purpose is shown full size in Fig. 4. It is worked by a fine screw, and easily measures to half a mil.

Another convenient way of designating the size of uncovered wire is by its weight per mile. This method is adopted to a large extent in the telegraph and telephone service.

Ohm-mile.—Multiplying the weight of one mile of wire of a certain material by its resistance a number is obtained which is constant for that material, and is known as the *Ohm-mile,* as it represents the weight of one mile of a wire of that material measuring one ohm

resistance.   The resistance of a mile of any other wire
of the same material can be at once found by dividing
the constant by its weight per mile, or its weight per
mile is obtained by dividing by its resistance per mile.

The constant for the hard-drawn copper wire used
for telephone lines is 892, or, roughly, 900. That for the
silicium bronze wire generally used for telephone lines
may be taken at 1950.

Copper Wire.—The following are very useful formulæ
for the calculation of resistance, etc., of *pure* copper
wires, the diameters being given in mils :—

1. The resistance per mile of a wire d mils in
dia. $= \frac{54892}{d^2}$

2. The weight per mile $= \frac{d^2}{63 \cdot 13}$

3. The dia. of a wire weighing n lbs. per mile $=$
$\sqrt{n \times 63 \cdot 13}$ mils.

4. From No. 1 the resistance of a wire one foot long,
and one mil dia. $= 10\cdot4$ ohms, from which is obtained :—

5. The resistance of a wire l feet in length and d mils
in dia. $= \frac{10\cdot4 \times l}{d^2}$ ohms.

If the wire is of any other metal than copper its
resistance may be obtained by multiplying the resistance obtained for a copper wire of equal size (by No. 1
or No. 4 formula), by the number giving the com-
parative resistance of the metal on page 10.

The above formulæ only hold good for wire at a
temperature of 60° F. or 15° C., but are sufficiently
accurate for rough purposes.

The Percentage Conductivity of any wire is the resistance of that wire compared with one of the same dimensions of pure copper at the same temperature. It is obtained by multiplying the calculated resistance of the pure copper wire by 100, and dividing the product by the actual measured resistance of the wire in question.

CHAPTER II.

BATTERIES USED IN TELEPHONY.

THE elementary facts in regard to voltaic cells, it is presumed, will be known to the reader, therefore practical points will be mostly referred to in connection with them.

The qualities which it is desirable a cell should possess may be summed up as follows:—

1. It should have a large E.M.F.
2. This should remain constant in working.
3. Its internal resistance should be small.
4. This also should be constant.
5. The materials it consumes should be cheap.
6. There should be no waste of these materials when the cell is not in use, that is, no *local action*.
7. Its condition should be capable of being easily inspected.
8. It should be easily refreshed.
9. It should not emit offensive fumes.
10. Its first cost should be small.

No one cell is known which unites in itself all the

above qualities. Each cell has its special advantages; so it becomes a practical question to decide which are the most important conditions necessary for any particular purpose.

For ordinary telephone work the most important qualities are Nos. 5, 6, and 9; but Nos. 1, 7, 8, and 10 are also of importance. No cell has yet been found which unites these qualities so well as the Leclanché, which, therefore, is almost universally used for telephonic purposes. Its only fault is that it is deficient in constancy when heavily worked.

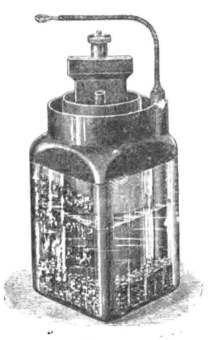

Fig. 5.

Polarization.—The different kinds of cells in use represent so many methods of preventing *polarization*, caused by a deposit of hydrogen gas on the electro-negative plate, which increases the resistance of the cell, and opposes the original current, by tending to send one in the opposite direction.

The Leclanché Cell.—The ordinary form is made up of a glass vessel of the shape shown in Fig. 5. Into this a zinc rod, provided with a connecting wire, is placed. Inside the glass vessel is a cylindrical pot of porous earthenware containing a carbon plate, round which is packed a mixture of about equal parts of carbon and needle binoxide of manganese broken into pieces of about the size of peas, care being taken to prevent dust being included. The carbon plate is provided with a lead cap and terminal.

To set in action, the glass is nearly filled with a saturated solution of sal-ammoniac or chloride of ammonium. This gradually percolates through the porous pot, until the whole is left about three-fourths full.

The action which takes place, under favourable conditions, is as follows :—The zinc combines with the chlorine of the sal-ammoniac to form zinc chloride, which is dissolved in the solution, whilst the hydrogen set free from the sal-ammoniac robs the binoxide of manganese of some of its oxygen to form water ; ammonia being also given off, as shown in the chemical formula :—

$$Zn + 2NH_4Cl + 2MnO_2 = ZnCl + H_2O + 2NH_3 + Mn_2O_3$$

If the cell is hard worked the action becomes more complicated, substances, such as oxy-chlorides of zinc, being formed which are with difficulty dissolved in the solution, and soon impair the working and lead to the polarization of the cell. On allowing it to rest, however, it quickly regains its power.

One of the best features of the Leclanché cell is that no *local action* or waste of materials takes place when not in use, unless impure zinc is used. The ammonia gas given off during action is not offensive and is seldom noticed, unless the cell is very hard worked.

There are many practical points in connection with the cell to which attention should be paid.

Carbon Plate.—The attachment of the lead cap to the carbon is one of the most important points, and much trouble was at one time experienced by the solution creeping up through the pores of the carbon and acting upon the lead and the terminal. This quickly corroded and destroyed the connection. To prevent this action, about two inches of the top of the carbon should be soaked for some time in hot paraffin wax. This plugs up the pores so that the creeping cannot take place. To ensure a good connection between the terminal and the carbon, the latter should have two or three holes of about $\frac{1}{4}$ dia. drilled at about $\frac{3}{16}$ in. from its top edge, and the shank of the terminal should be tinned before the lead is cast round it and the head of the carbon.

The terminals, if made of brass, are apt to be corroded by the ammonia fumes and by solution dropped on them accidentally. No such corrosion takes place if the terminals are made of Britannia metal.

The top of the porous pot should also be soaked in paraffin, and the carbon block and mixture kept in place by a covering of marine glue about $\frac{1}{4}$ in. thick, in which two small ventilating holes are made. The holes are useful also for pouring a little of the solution in the pot when the cell is required to work at once.

The porous pots should be rather soft, as hard ones offer too great a resistance to give sufficient current for a transmitter, but will do for a ringing battery.

Only the best needle manganese should be used, or

the cells will soon give out. It is desirable, therefore, to get the cells from the best makers, who only use first-class materials. The same applies to the sal-ammoniac used, as impurities in this give rise to local action.

The zinc rod is best made of rolled metal, and care should be taken that its wire connection is well soldered.

The glass cell should be coated at its top for a distance of about 2 inches inside and out with black Japan varnish, to prevent the solution from creeping over the edge of the jar and down the outside by capillary action. The cell is often drained dry in this way to the detriment of wall-paper, etc., in the offices where it is fixed. The solution will not wet the varnish, and so the creeping is prevented. Paraffin wax is sometimes used for the purpose, but is not nearly so effective. The lead cap and top of carbon should also be varnished.

The cells are made in three sizes. The No. 2, or medium, is the one mostly used ; but the No. 1, or largest size, is frequently employed for the working of trans-mitters with much advantage, as they are heavily worked, and a greater body of depolarizing material is desirable and more solution to keep up its strength. A stronger current is also obtained, as the internal resistance is only about 1 to 2 ohms as compared with that of the No. 2, which is from 2 to 4 ohms.

The E.M.F. of the Leclanché = 1·46 volts at starting.

The Agglomerate Leclanché.—In order to get rid of the porous pot and its resistance, a mixture of carbon and binoxide of manganese is solidified by being crushed and mixed with a proportion of gum-lac resin, and the resulting compound put into moulds, and subjected to a great pressure after being heated to 212° F. The solid blocks thus formed are fastened round the carbon-plate by india-rubber bands, usually provided with small

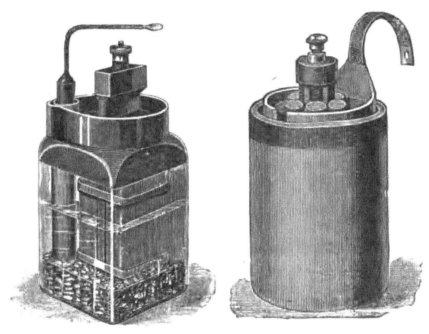

Fig. 6.   Fig. 7.

holes for the zinc rods to keep the latter from touching the blocks. For the same purpose, and also to prevent the cell running down too quickly, small porous pots are sometimes provided for the zincs, as shown in Fig. 6.

Fig. 7 shows a later form, called the *six-block agglo-merate* cell. A fluted carbon block is used, to

D

which are bound six cylindrical agglomerate blocks, completely protecting the carbon from direct action. With it may be used a cylindrical zinc surrounding the blocks, and very materially reducing the internal resistance of the cell.

The expectation that these agglomerate cells would altogether supplant the porous pot form has not been realised, as they have not proved so reliable. They are, however, used in preference when specially strong currents are required.

The Daniell Cell.—In the matter of constancy no working cell is superior to the Daniell. Except by the British Post Office, it is not used for the general working of telephones, but is frequently used for the special purpose of working the transmitters in very busy telephonic exchanges, especially where the multiple switch-board is employed.

The ordinary Daniell is made up of a copper-plate or cylinder immersed in a saturated solution of sulphate of copper, which is separated by porous earthenware from a vessel containing a zinc plate or cylinder immersed in a weak solution of sulphate of zinc. The hydrogen, instead of polarizing the cell, acts upon the sulphate of copper, and metallic copper from this is deposited on the copper-plate.

The defects of the Daniell are that its internal resistance is high, and that the fluids get mixed through the division. Much local action results, and it is no advantage to disconnect the cell from its work to recuperate.

To remedy these defects to some extent, advantage has been taken of the fact that the specific gravity of a saturated solution of sulphate of copper is greater than that of a weak solution of sulphate of zinc, to form what are called *Gravity Cells*. Two of what are called the *Crowfoot* gravity cells are shown in Fig. 8. The glass cells are 6½ in. dia. and 8¼ in. deep. Three copper strips, about 2 in. wide, are rivetted together by a copper

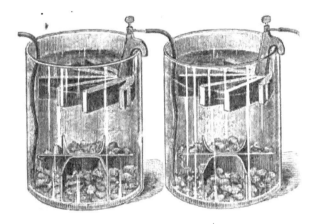

Fig. 8.

rivet, and then opened out into the shape shown at the bottom, a gutta-percha covered wire being attached for connection. The jar is next filled three-parts full of water, and crystals of sulphate of copper are dropped in until the copper is nearly covered, and then a solution of sulphate of zinc is carefully put in the top of the jar. Lastly, the crowfoot-shaped zinc is hung on the side of the jar, as shown. Another form of gravity cell is shown in Fig. 9.

Much attention needs to be paid to these cells, for if the solution of sulphate of zinc gets too strong, it becomes heavier than the sulphate of copper solution, and sinks to the bottom, and the displaced copper solution deposits copper on the zinc. Some of the top liquid should therefore be taken out every few days by

Fig. 9.

means of a syringe, and water put in to take its place. A hydrometer is a very useful instrument to indicate the degree of saturation of the upper solution. More copper crystals should be dropped through the liquid as the others are dissolved. The cells must be kept very still, or the solutions will mix.

The E.M.F. being only 1·065 volts, two cells joined up in series are required to work a Blake transmitter.

Other batteries are used occasionally in telephony, such as Fuller's Bichromate of Potash, for very strong currents; Bennett's Iron-borings, and Clark's Silver Chloride.

Dry Cells.—Some forms of dry cells, such as the Silvertown, Gassner and the Hellesen, are extending in use for special purposes, such as for use with portable telephone sets for testing lines. The last-named cell appears to be the best of the class, giving very satis - factory results, and is comparatively cheap. Its E.M.F. = 1·4 volts, and the internal resistance of a cell about the size of a No. 2 Leclanché is only about $\frac{1}{10}$th of an ohm, so that a powerful current can be obtained from it through a low resistance.

Battery Boxes.— These should be made so that both the front and top will open, in order that inspection of the cells may be easy. The cells should be prevented

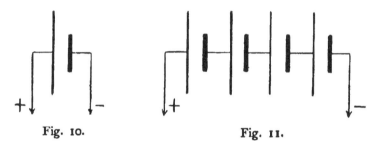

Fig. 10.   Fig. 11.

from touching each other, or the sides of the box, by a light wooden framework fitting between them.

In diagrams a cell is usually represented by two parallel lines, a short thick one for the zinc, and a longer thin one for the copper or carbon, as shown in Fig. 10. Batteries are represented by combinations of these, as Fig. 11, which shows a battery of four cells joined up *in series*.

The E.M.F. and internal resistance of such a com- bination will be four times that of a single cell. When a low internal resistance is required cells are joined up so that all the zincs are connected together, and all the carbons together, as in Fig. 12, which shows three cells so connected *abreast*, or for *quantity*, as it is called. The internal resistance of such a combination will be ⅓rd that of a single cell, but the E.M.F. will only be equal to that of a single cell, the combination

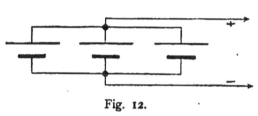

being only equivalent to a single cell having plates three times the size. It is much better to use large-sized cells, when they can be obtained, than to resort to the above arrangement.

Fig. 12.

Much valuable information in regard to batteries is given in Walker's "Electricity in our Homes and Workshops," published in the same series as the present book.

CHAPTER III.

HISTORY.

THE first electrical appliance to which the name *telephone* was attached was that invented by Philip Reis, in 1861. This, however, was only intended for the transmission of musical sounds, although it appears that on some occasions it was successful in transmitting spoken words, but in an accidental manner, the principles involved not being adequately known. These principles were first clearly explained by Prof. Graham Bell, in 1876, and, as he produced the first practical instrument he is generally credited with the invention of the telephone.

Reis's Telephone.—Although of little practical use, Reis's instrument is important from a historical point of view. Its working depends upon the fact that an iron rod, when magnetised by a current, gives out a ticking sound. If the current be interrupted very frequently and regularly, and the rod attached by its two ends to a sounding-board or box, a musical note will be produced of a pitch depending upon the frequency of the breaks in the current. Fig. 13 shows one of Reis's arrangements of this kind, which serves as the receiver. The cover D fitted over the coil *g* and rod *d d* serves to intensify the result.

The transmitter, Fig. 14, was more complicated. It was so arranged that the voice or a musical instrument sounded into the mouthpiece T should cause interruptions in the current in unison with the vibrations of the sound produced. To accomplish this a large circular opening on the top of the box K is closed in with a

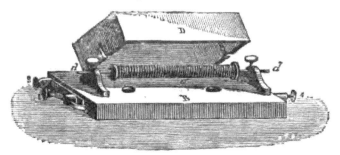

Fig. 13.

stretched membrane, *m*. On the upper surface of this is a strip of platinum, *o i*, connected to the terminal 2. On the part *o* of this in the centre of the membrane, one corner of a platinum point attached at *b* to an angle-shaped metal piece, *a b c*, just touches it under normal conditions. If the contact *o* forms part of a circuit which includes a battery and the receiver, Fig. 13, and the membrane be set in vibration by a musical sound, the circuit will be interrupted at every vibration. Each interruption produces a sound in the receiver, and a musical sound similar in pitch to the one sounded in

the mouthpiece of the transmitter will be given out by
the receiver, no matter how distant it may be. The
apparatus shown on the sides of the instruments are
battery keys for signalling purposes.

By such means the *pitch* of any sound may be
reproduced at a distance, but this was not enough for
the transmission of speech. Pitch is only one of the
characteristics of sound, for besides it, sound has *quality*

Fig. 14.

or timbre, and degrees of *loudness or intensity*, which it
was necessary to transmit before human speech could be
perfectly transmitted. This cannot be done by an
apparatus which employs interrupted currents for its
working.

Sound is conveyed through air by a wave motion.
The wave motion of water is caused by an up-and-down
motion of the particles of water. Wave motion in air
is caused by a movement of the particles of air back-

wards and forwards *in a line with* the direction in which
the wave progresses. Every different sound needs a
different motion of the air particles for its conveyance,
and if the characteristic motion of any sound can be impressed upon the air particles at any place, that sound
will be reproduced.

This was the problem attacked by Prof. Bell. *Bell's
Telephone*, the instrument with which Prof. Bell first
succeeded, is shown in Fig. 15, where E is an electro-

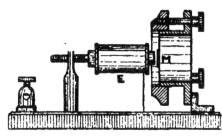

magnet mounted so as
to be adjustable near
the centre of a mem-
brane, M, of gold-beater's
skin, stretched over the
end of a hollow cylinder.
A small piece of clock-
spring is cemented to

Fig. 15.

the centre of the membrane. Two of these instruments, some distance apart, were joined in a circuit,
including a battery, one used as transmitter and
the other as receiver. The action was as follows:—
On speaking into the cylinder the membrane moved in
unison with the movements of the air particles. These
movements of a magnetic substance in front of the
magnet produced alterations in the magnet field in
which the coils were situated. The effect was to cause
electrical pulsations or waves to pass through the coils,
the connecting wires and the coils of the receiving
instrument at the distant end, of such a nature that
they so affected the attraction between the magnet and

the steel spring of the receiver as to set up exactly
corresponding movements in its diaphragm to those
impressed upon that of the transmitter. These movements being impressed upon the air, a person listening
at the end of the cylinder would hear the original sound

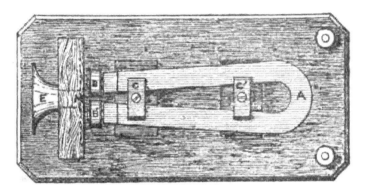

Fig. 16

Fig. 17.

reproduced, but in a much fainter degree. All the
characteristics of any sound could thus be transmitted
and reproduced.

Gradually improvements were made by Prof. Bell,
until he arrived at the instrument shown in Figs. 16 and
17, where a compound horse-shoe permanent magnet, A,

took the place of the original electro-magnet, two small coils of wire, B B', being fixed on soft iron pieces attached to its poles. It had been found that no battery was required, its only use being to produce a magnetic field by means of the electro-magnet. The gold-beater's skin membrane had also been discarded, one of thin sheet-iron being substituted.

With this instrument much louder effects were produced, but it lacked portability, to attain which the

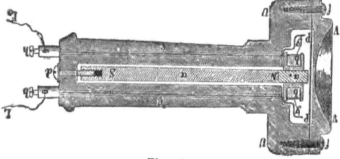

Fig. 18.

form shown in Fig. 18 was adopted, and may be considered the final form. It was made up of a wooden case in the handle part of which was fitted a bar magnet, N S. On one end of this magnet was fixed the bobbin of wire, *b b*, the ends of the coil being connected to the terminals at the end of the handle. The diaphragm, P P, of ferrotype iron clamped close in front of the end of the magnet by the cap V V, which was provided with a funnel-shaped mouth or ear-piece and a small orifice in the centre.

The action of the later forms is similar to that of the

original form, except that the pulsatory currents are wholly developed by the movements of the diaphragm, instead of the movement simply varying a current already existing.

The instruments served both as transmitters and receivers, and came extensively into use in this form. Lines were joined up, as shown in Fig. 19, but two instruments were generally used at each end to save the constant changing from mouth to ear, and *vice versâ.*

The received sounds, although very clear, were rather

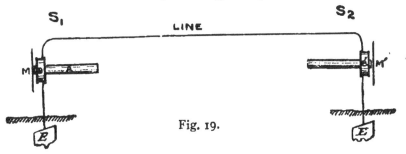

Fig. 19.

faint, so much so that the telephone would have come but slowly into general use, if an instrument to serve as a transmitter, based on a different principle and giving much louder sounds, had not shortly after been invented.

It had been pointed out by Prof. Bell that the necessary waves of electricity might be produced in another way than the one employed in his *magneto-telephone*, in which the waves were produced by a varying E.M.F. caused in the transmitter by the movement of the diaphragm. The second method of producing the waves was by *varying the resistance* in the circuit in proportion to the movements of the air-particles whilst the E.M.F. remained constant. Bell had shown a method of doing this by means of a platinum-wire attached to the centre of a horizontal stretched membrane, and just dipping under the surface of acidulated water. The wire and the water formed part of a circuit containing a receiver and a battery. On speaking to the membrane its vibrations would cause the extent of contact of the wire and water to be varied, and so produce corresponding variations and pulsations in the current circulating through the receiver, which latter would reproduce the sound in the manner already described.

On the same day that Bell filed his patent, Prof. E. Gray also filed one with similar suggestions for producing variations in the resistance of an electric circuit. The apparatus employed by the two inventors for this purpose were almost identical.

Edison's Carbon Transmitter.—Edison, in 1878, was the first to produce a successful instrument based on the variation of resistance principle. He took advantage of the fact discovered by Du Moncel, "that the increase of pressure between two conductors in contact produces a diminution in their electrical resistance." This is eminently the case with carbon, and this was the substance chosen by Edison, its great variation of resistance under pressure having been independently discovered by him.

The instrument he finally adopted after many were tried is shown in Fig. 20, where D is a vibrating disc of mica clamped to the iron case by the iron. cap, in which is screwed the ebonite mouthpiece E. Pressing against the centre of D is the ivory button *b*, attached to a small disc of platinum, B B. This forms the loose cover of a chamber, with ebonite sides, in which is placed a quantity of lamp black, I.

The amount of initial pressure on the lamp-black can be regulated by the screw V. The terminals of the instrument are connected one to B B and the other to

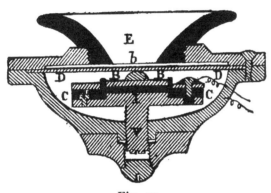

Fig. 20.

the metal case, the lamp-black thus forming part of the circuit.

Speaking on to the diaphragm causes it to vary its pressure on the carbon, producing corresponding variations in the resistance of a circuit containing also a Bell receiver and a battery. The pulsatory currents thus set up, passing through the receiver, give rise to a reproduction of words spoken into the transmitter. The received sounds are much louder with this instrument than when a magneto transmitter is used.

Induction Coil.—Edison still further augmented the power of the instrument, especially when used over long distances, by using an induction coil in conjunction with his transmitter. The carbon and battery were included in the primary wire circuit, and the line and receivers in the secondary circuit of fine wire. This subject will be referred to again in Chapter V.

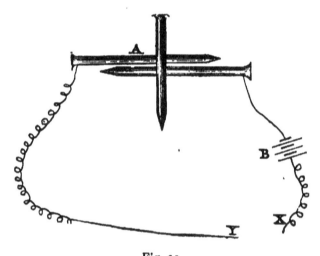

Fig. 21.

Microphones.—The next step in the direction of improvement was the discovery by Prof. Hughes, of London, in 1878, of the fact that *any loose contact* between conductors would act as a telephonic transmitter owing to the variations of resistance caused between them by the impact of the sound waves. The simple means he employed caused much astonishment. Three nails arranged as in Fig. 21, and joined up with a battery and a Bell receiver, were found to be sufficient to convey speech, and were even so sensitive as to render audible the most minute sounds, such as the walking of a fly, etc. The best effect was obtained with carbon in one shape or another, that given in Fig. 22 being one of the best forms. Two carbon blocks, C C′, have a cup-shaped hollow made in each, in which the carbon pencil A is loosely held;

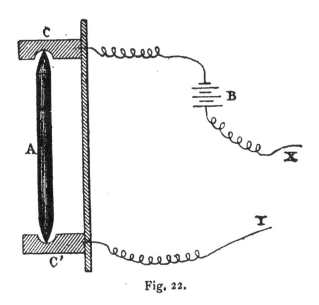

Fig. 22.

C C′ are attached to a sounding-board of thin deal, wires being connected to C C′ for joining up the battery and receiver. The complete instrument is shown in Fig. 23, and forms the parent of a very numerous class of telephone transmitters; indeed, nearly all transmitters in use are but modifications or amplifications of some form or other of Hughes's microphone.

E

Edison's Loud-Speaking Receiver.—This was a very interesting instrument, and was much used at one time. It was based on the fact discovered by Edison and utilized by him for the construction of a telegraphic instrument, that the friction between a metal and a substance capable of electrolytic action varies in proportion to the strength of a current passing through

Fig. 23.

the points of contact. The telephone-receiver constructed on this principle is shown in Fig. 24. A diaphragm of mica is mounted over an opening in a box, as shown, and a strip of platinum, C (only the end of which is shown), is attached to its centre and projects at right angles from it. The end of C lies flat on the surface of a chalk cylinder, A, which is moistened with a solution of some easily decomposed electrolyte, such as potassic iodide. The platinum strip C and the metal supports of A are connected in circuit with a battery and a carbon transmitter. On turning the cylinder by the handle W so that the top moves away from the mica disc, the friction (which can be regulated by the

Fig. 24.

screw E) will cause the centre of the disc to be pulled inwards. On a current passing the friction at the contact will be reduced in proportion to the strength of the current, and the disc will partly recover its position. On passing the undulatory currents from a transmitter through the contact and continuously rotating the cylinder the disc will be caused to vibrate, and will give out a sound similar to that sounded in the transmitter.

It was a very powerful instrument when properly adjusted, giving sounds capable of being heard by a large audience. The tone of the instrument left much to be desired, however. ¡This, and the necessity of keeping the cylinder moist and turning the handle, led to its discontinuance. The rod G being raised brought a small roller saturated with the solution from the reservoir T into contact with A in order to renew its moisture.

Many other interesting telephonic instruments have since been invented, such as Bell & Tainter's photo-phone, in which the fact that some substances, such as selenium, have their electrical resistance affected by light is utilised to construct an instrument worked by light falling on an arrangement of selenium included in a circuit with a Bell receiver. In Tainter's radiophone the same effect is produced by heat rays, and in the thermo-telephone of W. H. Preece the expansions and contractions caused in a wire by the undulatory currents from a transmitter are utilised to produce a receiving instrument. For further particulars of the instruments mentioned, the reader is referred to Preece & Maier's book, " The Telephone."

Dolbear has produced a receiver which works on the principle of the condenser. The charged coatings, one of which forms the diaphragm of the instrument, exert more or less attraction on each other, according to the difference of potential to which they are charged. The potential is varied by connection to a telephone transmitter and battery.

Telephonic Exchanges.—The telephone at first was used almost exclusively for private purposes, but very early it was recognised by Mr. Hubbard, the father-in-law of Prof. Bell, that its usefulness would be greatly enhanced by the establishment of *telephonic exchanges*. Each member who joined one of these had to pay a certain subscription, for which he was supplied with a set of telephonic instruments and a line wire which joined him up to a *central office*, where *switch-boards* were fixed and operators in attendance to connect the line of any one subscriber to that of any other one, so that they might converse together.

The first telephonic exchange was established in Boston, U.S.A., in May, 1877. In this country they were not established until the latter part of 1879, when the invention of the microphone had greatly extended the practical usefulness of the telephone.

Very few towns in civilized countries are now without their telephonic exchange, and in most large towns business would be completely disorganised by the cessation of its advantages for a few days.

CHAPTER IV.

RECEIVERS IN GENERAL USE.

The Bell Receiver.—The form of receiver universally used by the telephone companies in this country until a few months ago is shown in section in Fig. 25, about two-thirds full size. The dimensions of the different parts are given in millimetres. The permanent magnet is a compound one, made up of four thin bars, provided with pole-pieces of soft iron, as shown in the side view, Fig. 26.

On one of the pole-pieces is a small boxwood bobbin, wound with silk-covered copper wire of 5 mils diameter to a resistance of about 75 ohms.

The case is of polished ebonite, provided with a screw cap, and the ends of the coil are connected to thick covered wires attached to the terminals at the end of the handles.

This instrument held its own for a number of years, and proved its superiority for simplicity and efficiency against many competing instruments. It is now, however, giving way to smaller and lighter ones, more convenient to handle.

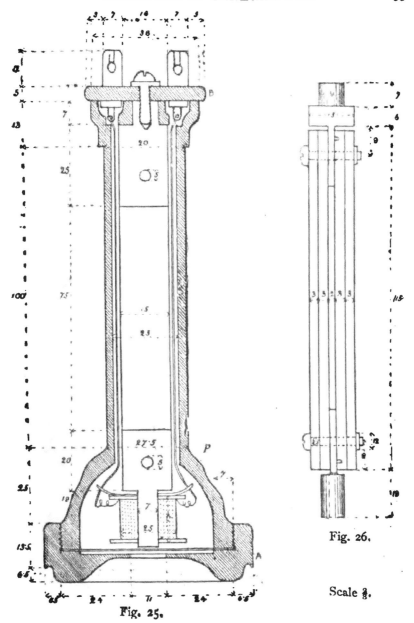

Fig. 25.

Fig. 26.

Scale ⅜.

The Gower Receiver.—This has been extensively used by the British Post Office authorities and by many of our railway companies. It is more powerful than the Bell, but is more cumbrous. Its points of

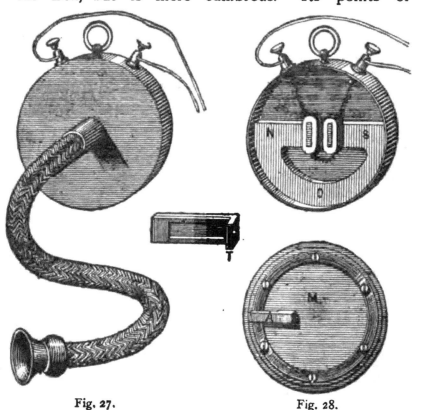

Fig. 27.   Fig. 28.

difference are that it has a larger and thicker diaphragm (about 4¼ inches as compared with 2¼ inches diameter), a powerful horse-shoe magnet of the shape shown in Fig. 28, the two poles of which are brought close together, and each furnished with a flat, soft iron pole-piece, on which is fixed a flat coil of wire. The magnet is placed inside a shallow brass box, furnished with two binding screws, to which the coils, which are joined up in series, are connected.

The diaphragm of tinned iron is clamped in the lid of the box by a brass ring and screws, as shown at M. On the other side of the diaphragm a brass tube is fixed, into which a flexible tube with mouth or ear-piece is inserted (Fig. 27), or, in place of this, a Y tube is often connected with two flexible tubes. The coils are wound to a resistance of 100 ohms each.

An attachment used in the early days, when the instrument served both as transmitter and receiver, is shown at A, and on a larger scale at L T, Fig. 28. It was for the purpose of signalling from one station to another, and consisted of a flat tube bent at right angles, furnished with a vibrating reed. On blowing into the flexible tube this reed was set in vibration, and caused corresponding vibrations in the diaphragm, producing powerful pulsatory currents, which, passing through the instrument at the other end, set its diaphragm in powerful vibration, making sufficient noise to call attention.

From the dimensions given it will be evident that the instrument is too heavy and bulky to put to the ear, and the consequent necessity of using flexible tubes detracts considerably from its effectiveness, as they enclose a large body of air, all of which has to be set in vibration, the amplitude of the vibrations which reach the ear being thereby lessened.

Ader Receiver.—This was invented by M. Ader, of Paris, and has been very extensively used in France and Belgium, and has everywhere given great satisfaction.

In the Ader a new feature is introduced to enhance the effect of the magnet. To illustrate the speciality, a model was shown at the Paris Electrical Exhibition in 1881. It consisted of a permanent magnet, with a sheet-iron armature arranged in front of its poles, but kept a short distance apart by a spring. On sliding a block of soft iron up behind the armature, the latter was attracted to the poles, showing that the mass of iron behind had strengthened the action of the magnet on the armature by apparently concentrating the lines of force upon it.

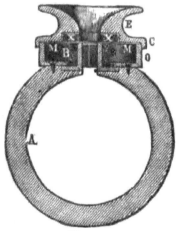

Fig. 29.

This principle was introduced in the Ader receiver by using a soft iron ring, or washer, let into the cap of the instrument, as shown at X X in Fig. 29. A circular magnet, A, is used, both poles, B B, being provided with two flat coils, like the Gower, and wound to about the same resistance. A metal box, M M, is screwed to the magnet, as shown, and is provided with an ebonite cap and ear-piece.

A modified form of Ader has recently come into use

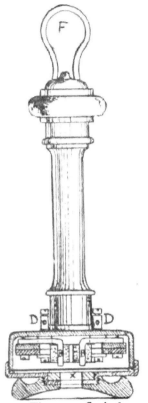

in this country, and has proved to be superior to most Bell receivers, being also smaller and handier.

The only important difference is in the shape and size of the magnet, which is altogether enclosed in the metal box, as shown in Fig. 30, to a scale of one-half.

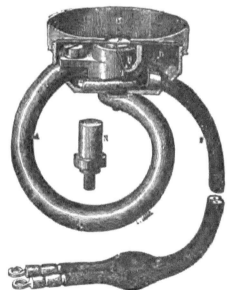

Fig. 30.—Scale ½.

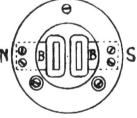

Fig. 31.—Scale ¼.

Fig. 32.—Scale ¼.

The novel form of magnet adopted is shown separately in Fig. 31. It is of a circular form, made up of two thin rings of steel, fastened together and magnetised across one of their diameters N S, two soft iron pole pieces, B B, being screwed to these points and brought to the centre, where they are furnished with flat coils. These are joined in series, and the two free ends brought out through ivory bushes in the case and attached to the binding posts D D. A wooden handle, with loop, F, is attached.

D'Arsonval Receiver.—In the Gower and Ader both poles of the magnet are used, each fitted with a coil ; in the D'Arsonval both poles are utilized, but only one coil. As shown in Fig. 32, one pole is furnished with a round coil, B, and the other is attached to a soft-iron cylinder, T, which fits over it, thus forming a box electro-magnet, which concentrates the lines of force due to the operating currents and the magnet in the centre of the diaphragm.

The core N, shown separately, screws into the pole of the magnet, and also serves as clamping screw to secure the box D.

Siemens' Receiver.—This instrument is the one chiefly used in Germany, and a remarkable testimony to its excellence is the fact that up to the year 1888 it served both as transmitter and receiver to the exclusion of carbon transmitters.

It differs only in shape from the Gower. Fig. 34 shows the internal parts, and Fig. 33 the outer case in which they are fixed : *m m* is a powerful horse-shoe magnet, with coils, *u u*; *r r* are connecting wires to terminals on wooden blocks *i*, and *v* an adjusting screw ; *g g* is the loop for hanging up the instrument ; *e e* in both figures is the base of the instrument.

The instrument shown is much larger than the

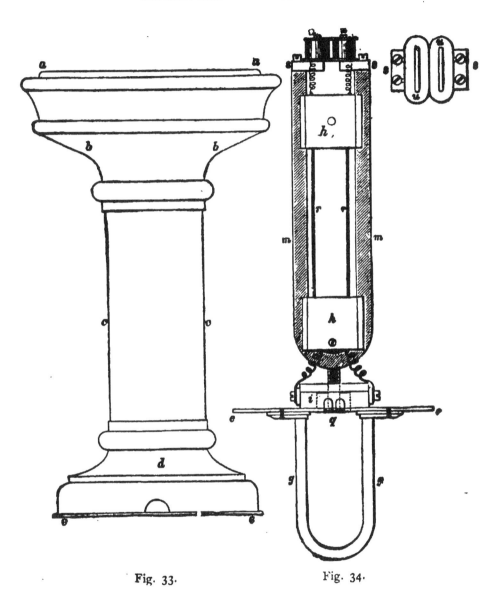

Fig. 33.   Fig. 34.

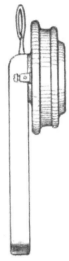

Fig. 35.

Bell, but many receivers are now being introduced of the Siemens' form, called *double polar receivers,* the magnets of which are enclosed in similar cases to the Bell or even smaller ones.

Another form of Siemens' receiver, Fig. 35, is now much used, in which the pole-pieces and coils are fixed on the sides of the magnet, instead of at the ends. The magnet is wrapped with leather, and is grasped by the hand in using.

The Watch Receiver. — This is a double pole receiver of a neat and compact form, being only about the size of an ordinary watch. It is the type of a numerous class of small instruments. Fig. 36 gives a view of its inside construction : A is a block of vulcanite on which the terminals are fixed, the conducting wires are taken out through holes in the metal case, being protected from contact or fraying by being enclosed in india-rubber tubes.

Fig. 36.—Scale ⅜.

Relation between strength of magnet and size of Dia-

phragm.—Mercadier has conducted a series of experiments having for their object the determination of the above problem. From these experiments he has arrived at the following conclusions :—

1. For every telephone of a given magnetic field there is a thickness of diaphragm which gives a maximum effect. The stronger the magnet the thicker should be the diaphragm.

2. The thickness of diaphragm being known for a certain magnetic field, there is one diameter for the diaphragm which gives the best result. This diameter will be greater the stronger the magnetic field.

3. That arrangement of magnet and coils will give the best result in which the greatest number of lines of force run through the coil in a direction at right angles to the plane of the coil, and in which these vary most with any movement of the diaphragm.

CHAPTER V.

TRANSMITTERS IN PRACTICAL USE.

As before stated, the transmitters now used are all based upon some form of Prof. Hughes's microphone.

They may be roughly divided into three classes:— 1, the Metal and Carbon; 2, the Pencil Carbon; and 3, the Granulated Carbon.

The prototype of the first class is the Blake, of the second the Crossley, and of the third the Hunnings.

Blake's Transmitter.—This is probably the most important of all, judging at any rate by the number in use. It was invented soon after the microphone, and was at once adopted by all the Bell Telephone companies, and is still almost exclusively used for all exchange work in America and this country. When properly made and adjusted, it probably gives a purer and more perfect reproduction of the voice than any other. It has the demerit of requiring adjustment at times, and, as a rule, is not sufficiently powerful for long-distance talking. Fig. 37 shows the inside of the instrument when open, and Fig. 38 a section through the centre of

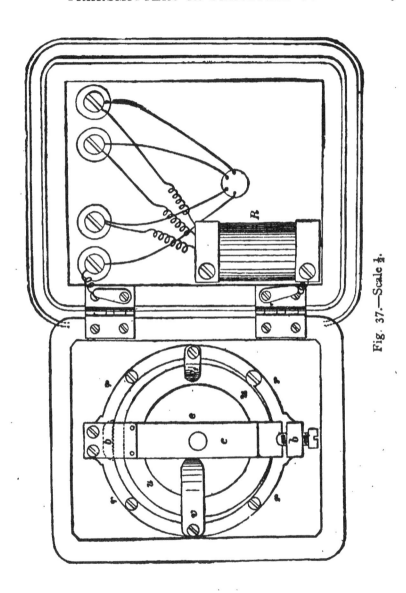

Fig. 37.—Scale ½.

F

the transmitter proper, which is fixed on the door of a small box. The framework is a brass or iron casting, forming a ring, *r r*, with projections, *b b*, at top and bottom. Into a recess in this ring the sheet-iron diaphragm *e* is inserted, its edge being clipped by an

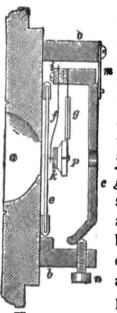

indiarubber ring, *u u*. The diaphragm is kept in position by a clip, *v*, bearing on the india-rubber ring, and by a spring, *v*, which presses nearer its centre, being insulated from it by a pad of felt or india-rubber. To the top projection, *b*, an arm, *c*, is attached by means of the spring *m* and screws. To a projection of this arm a small steel spring, *g*, and a very slender german-silver spring, *f*, are clamped by two screws at *i*. The spring *f* is carefully insulated by being clamped between two pieces of vulcanite. It has at its extremity a small pellet of platinum, which presses against the centre of the diaphragm on one side, and against a round button of hard carbon let into a brass socket, *p*, on the other. This brass piece is attached by a screw to the end of the spring *g*.

Fig. 38.—Scale ½.

The spring *m* tends to throw the arm *c* from the diaphragm. Its distance therefrom, and the consequent pressure of the carbon button on the platinum pellet is regulated by the screw *n* pressing against the lower part of the arm *c*.

The circuit through the instrument is made by connecting f to one of the hinges, and $r\,r$ to the other. The flat springs on the hinges ensure a good contact, the hinges themselves being apt to fail in this respect.

One of the hinges is connected to the left-hand one of the four terminals provided, and the other to one end of the primary wire of an induction coil, R, the other end of the coil being connected to the second terminal. Between these terminals a Leclanché cell is connected when the instrument is to be used, the other two terminals on the right being connected through a switch to the line and instruments at the other end.

Use of Induction Coil.—The working of a microphone depends upon the variation of the resistance of the circuit in which it is included when the sound waves impinge upon it. The greater this variation, the more intense will be the reproduced sound. The variation will be relatively greater the lower the total resistance of the circuit. Therefore, to attain the greatest efficiency the total resistance of the circuit must be kept as low as possible. It follows that the efficiency will decrease as the distance transmitted increases if it is done directly. For example, the resistance of a Blake carbon after adjustment is about 5 ohms, and the variation caused by a certain sound may be 1 ohm; assume the rest of the circuit to be 15 ohms, and the variation would then be $\frac{1}{20}$ of the whole, but if the total resistance had been 1,000 ohms, a variation of only $\frac{1}{1000}$ would have been obtained, and the relative effect on the same receiver would not have been more than $\frac{1}{50}$ of that in the first case. An increase of battery would, to a certain extent, restore the power, but would be costly and troublesome.

By using an induction coil, and including the microphone and battery in the primary circuit of thick wire, its circuit resistance may be kept very low, and the relative variation will then be great. By making the secondary coil of a great number of turns of wire, the currents induced in it by the variations in the primary will have a high E.M.F., and will be able to overcome much resistance in the line and instruments at the other end with comparatively little loss of strength.

Figs. 37 and 38 are drawn to a scale of one-half. The diaphragm is $2\frac{3}{4}$ in.dia., and 19 mils thick. Resistance of induction coil:—primary, ·5 ohms; secondary, 175 ohms.

It should be understood that the inertia of the brass piece p is the secret of the Blake's action, it being too heavy to follow the very rapid movements of the diaphragm, and the carbon is subjected to great variations of pressure in consequence.

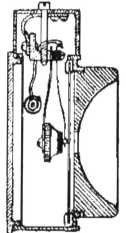

Metal-cased Blake.—Figs. 39 and 40 represent a form of Blake fitted in a round nickel-plated metal case, designed for use with switch-boards. Being much smaller than the ordinary form, it does not hide so large a part of the board from the operators. The general arrangement is the same, only the adjustment is managed rather differently. The instrument is sus-

Fig. 39.—Scale $\frac{1}{4}$.

pended by two flexible conductors, which pass through
insulating bushes in the case, and are attached to
terminals inside, one of which is insulated. The induction
coil is not contained in the
case, but is fixed in any convenient position near.

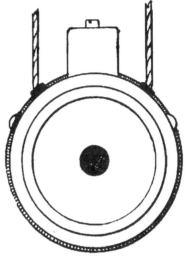

*Transmitter of the Société
des Téléphones.* — This is a
kind of double Blake, in which
the effects produced by the
movement of the diaphragm
are doubled. Fig. 41 is a
diagram of its connections:—
$a\,a$ is the diaphragm, b is a
block of carbon fixed in the
centre, c is another carbon
block rigidly attached to b by

Fig. 40.—Scale ½.

the non-conducting half ring d. An arm balanced on
a pivot carries on one end a counterweight, and on the
other a cone-shaped piece of platinised metal, e, which
fits between the carbon blocks b and c. The induction
coil J is made up of
three wires, two
primary and one
secondary. One end
of one of the primary
coils is connected to
b, and the opposite
end of the second
primary to c, the two

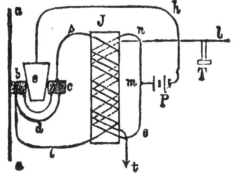

Fig. 41

free ends being connected together and to a battery, the other pole of which is connected to *e*. Any movement of the diaphragm will cause an increase of pressure of the piece *e* (which is practically a fixture) on one carbon and a diminution of pressure on the other, so that a current flowing through the former will be increased, and through the latter diminished. The currents passing in opposite directions through the two primary coils will both have the same effect on the secondary coil, producing an induced current of double strength. Every variation caused by the movement of the diaphragm will have a similar effect, so that the transmitting power of the instrument should be double that of the Blake. It is certainly more powerful, but the tone of the instrument is not so good as the Blake.

Pencil Microphones.—These are simply a number of Hughes's carbon pencils arranged and joined up in various ways. The tendency has been to gradually increase the number of pencils used, these being joined up in multiple circuit, so as to reduce the resistance and give a more equable result. This form of transmitter has the advantage of not requiring adjustment.

The Crossley was the first of the class brought into practical use, and it is still used to a considerable extent by the railway companies. As shown in Figs. 42 and 43, it consists of a deal board, DD, about ⅛th of an inch in thickness, on which are cemented four carbon blocks, B B′ B″ B‴. Between these are four carbon pencils, C C′ C″ C‴, whose ends have been turned down so as to fit loosely into holes in the blocks. The

board D D is glued by its four corners to four cork
pads, which are also attached to F H, forming the
sloping lid of a box containing the induction coil,

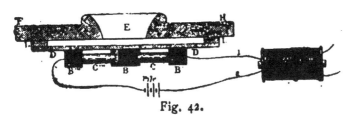

Fig. 42.

switches, etc ; E is a funnel-shaped opening, into which
the voice is directed. The connections to the induction
coil and battery (which generally consists of three or
four Leclanché cells) are shown in the figure. It will

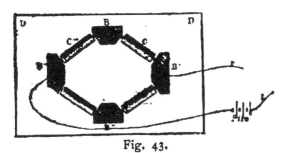

Fig. 43.

be seen that the current divides into two branches
having two pencils in each. The instrument is not so
powerful as others of the class, owing probably to the
high resistance of the primary circuit.

Ader's Transmitter.—This, as shown in Figs. 44 and
45, is somewhat similar to the Crossley, but has twelve
pencils in place of four, giving a resistance of only about
one-third.

The pine board on to which the blocks B B' B" are cemented is varnished on the opposite side, and has strips of india-rubber, C C', cemented round its edges, by which it is fastened so as to form a cover to an opening

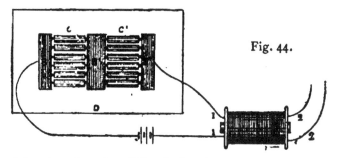

Fig. 44.

formed in the slanting lid of the instrument case. The person using the instrument simply directs his voice on to the varnished board.

Fig. 45.

The Ader is used extensively in France, and gives very good results.

The Gower.—The pencils of this transmitter are eight in number, radiating from a central block to other carbon blocks arranged in the form of an octagon, as shown in Fig. 46. The outside blocks are divided into two sets of four, each set being joined by copper pieces, S and S', to which the connections are made. One of the pencils is shown full size. The whole is fixed on a pine board, 9 in. by 5 in. by ⅛ in. thick, fixed in a box similar to that of the Crossley, except that a porcelain mouthpiece is

now used.   The pine board was formerly open like the
Ader, the voice being directed
on to it.

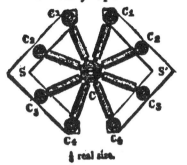

¼ real size.

Many thousands of these
instruments are in use in this
country.   It was adopted
from the first by the British
Post Office, and is looked
upon as a powerful instrument.

D'Arsonval's.—The pecu-
liarity of this pencil instrument is that it is capable

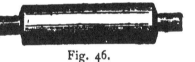

Fig. 46.

of adjustment.   This is managed in an   ingenious

manner.   Fig. 47 gives a
back view, and Fig. 48 a
section of the instrument :—
D is the pine board in this
case fixed upright.   Each
of the four carbon pencils
C C' C" C''' is encased in
a thin sheet-iron jacket,
F F' F" F'''.   A horse-shoe
magnet, A, is arranged behind
the pencils as shown by the
dotted outline, and can be
brought near or withdrawn
from them by a screw not
shown.   The nearer the
magnet is to the pencils

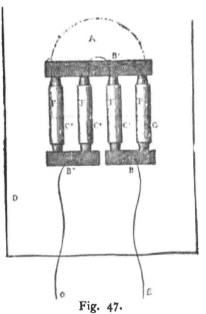

Fig. 47.

the less sensitive will be the instrument, owing to the increased pressure at the carbon contacts.

De Jongh's.—This is a novel form of instrument which has come extensively into use. Fig. 49 gives a section about half-full size :—D is the diaphragm clamped in position by the front of the case. On D are fixed, some distance apart, two sets of four carbon blocks, one set being shown at B B' B" B'". The blocks of each set are connected together by wire wound round them, and connected to a terminal as shown. Two rows of brass pins are driven into the back of the instrument in a slanting position, as at

Fig. 48. P P' P" P'", which shows half the number. On each pair of these pins is placed a long carbon pencil, shown in section at C C' C" C'", one being also shown separately at C. These would roll off the pins only that they are stopped by the carbon blocks. In this way the microphonic contact is made, the two sets of blocks being joined to a battery and a primary wire of an induction coil.

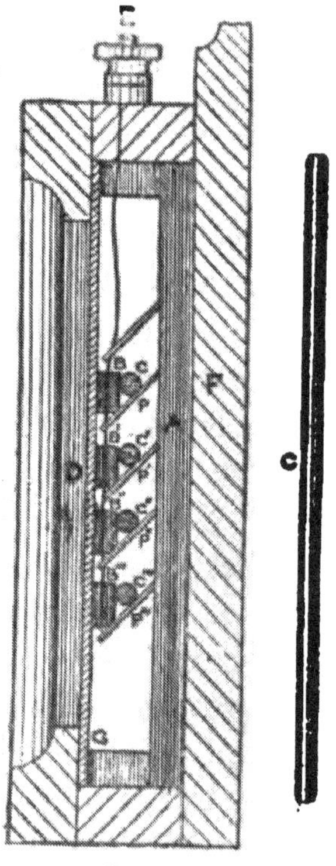

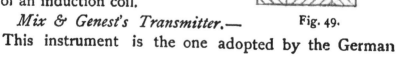

Fig. 49.

Mix & Genest's Transmitter.— This instrument is the one adopted by the German

Post Office, and a great deal has been heard of it in this country recently. The novelty is in the means taken to prevent the rasping sound often heard in pencil microphones, due to the pencils rolling in their loose bearing

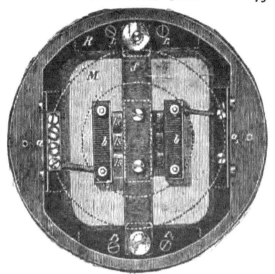

Fig. 50.—Scale ½.

holes. The pencils are held up to their work and pre-vented from rolling by being pressed up from behind by means of a soft pad. In Figs. 50 and 51, *b b* are two carbon blocks fixed to the pine wood diaphragm M, and *k k k* three carbon pencils of the ordinary kind, having behind them a soft pad of felt, *d*, mounted on a brass plate, which is itself mounted on a spring, *f*, capable of adjustment. The frame and mouthpiece T is of cast-iron.

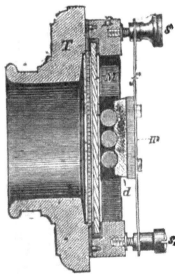

Fig. 51.—Scale ½.

Granulated Carbon Trans-mitters.—These are undoubtedly the most powerful for long-distance work.   They possess a very piercing quality of sound, which seems to carry better than the tones from other forms of transmitters.   Many different forms are constructed, but all contain crushed retort carbon or oven-coke sifted through wire gauze, so as to obtain even grains of about the size of those of fine gunpowder.   A quantity of this is enclosed in a cell with a flexible diaphragm.   Some forms have the drawback that the carbon tends to settle down and, to a certain degree, consolidate, and require to be shaken up now and then.   On account of the number of loose contacts the variation of resistance is very great, which explains their power.   Sometimes the granules are impregnated with mercury to lessen their resistance.

The Hunnings Transmitter.—This was the first of the type.   It is made up of a round wooden case, about 3 in.

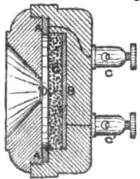

in diameter, shown in section in Fig. 52, to about half natural size. In the bottom of a recess, G, turned in it, a thin plate of carbon, B, is cemented, a wire connecting it to terminal C'.   At the front of the recess a platinum foil diaphragm, D, is clamped by the brass ring A A and screws ; A A

Fig. 52.—Scale ½.   is connected to terminal C.   The recess formed is filled about three-fourths full of the carbon granules.   A cap with a funnel mouthpiece is then screwed on, as shown.   The bottom of the funnel has generally a piece of wire gauze or crossed wires fixed over it, to prevent the foil being damaged by thoughtless persons poking it with pencils, etc. The instrument is generally held in the hand in using, and can therefore be easily shaken to prevent consolidation. It was at first used without an induction coil, but works much better with one.

The Moseley.—Instead of a platinum diaphragm, the Moseley has one of thin pine wood, in the centre of which is cemented a thin block of carbon, connected by fine wire to one of the terminals. The front of the diaphragm must be varnished to prevent the absorption of moisture, the amount of which, in consequence of having to put the instrument close to the mouth in using, is rather large, and is a decided drawback to this class of transmitter. Instead of holding it in the hand when using, the instrument is often mounted on a block by means of a dovetail wedge arrangement, which makes the connections, and enables the instrument to be removed for shaking when necessary.

Marr's Inertia Transmitter.—This wonderful little instrument was introduced by the late Mr. Charles Moseley for the purpose of transmitting operatic performances from the Manchester theatres, and proved a remarkable success not only for that purpose, but as a long-distance transmitter; its performances in the latter respect being superior to the best known forms of transmitters experimented with by the writer.

Fig. 53 gives a section of the instrument. The diaphragm and brass frame are similar to that of a Blake, but they are mounted in a round wooden case :—C is a small brass frame, on one face of which is cemented a piece

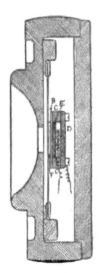

of sheet india-rubber, B. On the centre of this is cemented a piece of carbon, E, of such a size as just to fit easily inside C, but prevented from touching by the latter being lined with thin paper. On the opposite side of B, a small piece of cardboard, F, same size as the carbon E, is glued, by means of which the whole is glued to the diaphragm. The brass cell is closed in on the other side by a block of carbon, D, fixed to it by small screws. The space left between the carbons being filled three-fourths full with carbon granules. The cell is fixed to the diaphragm, about $\frac{1}{2}$ in. above its centre.

Fig. 53.—Scale $\frac{1}{2}$.

The instrument works on the inertia principle, the heavy

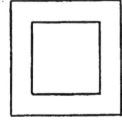

brass piece, a full-sized view of which is given in Fig. 54, remaining practically stationary, whilst the flexible india-rubber B allows the carbon block E to vibrate with the diaphragm.

The Berthon is another modification of the Hunnings, the foil diaphragm being replaced by a thin carbon disc. Between two carbon

Fig. 54.

discs, P P (Fig. 55), is formed a sort of truncated conical cell, C, three-fourths full of granules. The plates are

separated from each other and from the ebonite case A
by india-rubber rings, B B' *e*, the whole being kept
together by a brass ring, D. The round holes in the
case are to allow the air to escape, so as not to

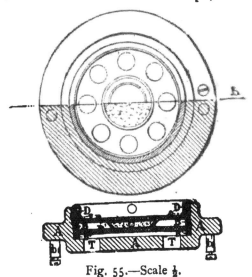

Fig. 55.—Scale ½.

impede the vibrations. The Berthon is much
used in France, especially' for switch-room
service.

The Roulez appears to have been very successful on the London-Paris line. The vibrating diaphragm is a carbon plate 4 inches in
diameter, to which is attached a light block of
wood carbon 2¼ inches long. A piece of
Bristol board is cemented between them,
as shown in Fig. 56. Three holes are
made into the block through the cardboard, and these are filled up with frag- Fig. 56.

ments of broken incandescent electric lamp filaments, through which the circuit is carried between the carbon block and the diaphragm.

The Berliner Universal.—The diaphragm of this is a carbon disc, D, Fig. 57, which is arranged in a horizontal

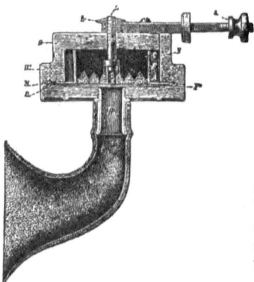

position with the granules above it. This arrangement is adopted in order to get over the difficulty of the granules settling down, as they are shaken up each time the instrument is used. The carbon disc is clamped down by the cover B, and a brass ring M, by which connection is made. A cylindrical

Fig. 57.—Scale ½.

space is formed by a wide felt ring, F, at the bottom of which the carbon granules are placed. Above, and just fitting the felt ring, is a cylindrical block of carbon, C, in the lower face of which a series of concentric conical grooves are turned. C is held in position and adjusted by the screwed pin L and terminal nut E. The head of L fits tightly into a hole bored in the carbon, and part of it is turned down, on to which part a short piece of india-rubber tubing, G (shown in section), fits and extends to the carbon disc, on which it lightly presses, serving to damp its vibrations.

Into a hole in the lower face of the wooden case B a brass tube, H, is screwed, on which fits the rubber funnel of the peculiar shape shown. The instrument is fitted to any case by two projecting bolts and nuts, only one of which is shown.

This is one of the best long-distance transmitters made, having a very piercing tone. Two No. 1 agglo-merate cells are generally used to it.

Thornberry's Long-Distance.—This is the one used

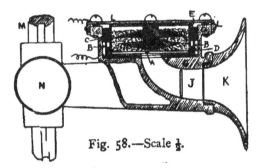

Fig. 58.—Scale ½.

most extensively for long-distance work in America. It is somewhat the same shape as the Berliner. Fig. 58 is a section to a scale of one-half. A is a platinum foil diaphragm, clamped at its edges in the shallow brass cylinder B B. Inside this, but insulated from it by the vulcanite rings C and D, is a brass cylindrical ring E, on the top of which rests a brass piece of the shape shown at F F, which reaches nearly to the diaphragm. The space around this is nearly filled with granules of coke, and the cell thus formed is placed in the recess made

G

in an iron casting, G. The bottom of G is fitted with an ebonite disc, in which two holes are made, one opening into the funnel J K, and the other for the passage outside of a terminal which is screwed into the brass box B. The casting is bushed with ebonite, to prevent contact with this terminal. The brass cap L, placed over the cell and screwed down on to it, makes contact with the brass piece F. The casting has a boss, which fits on to an iron rod, M, so that it may be adjusted in height and then clamped in position by the screw N. M is attached to an iron box which contains the induction coil.

The brass tray-light piece F maintains contact with the granules, relieves the foil of their weight, and reduces the resistance.

Comparison of Transmitters.—By using a very delicate dynamometer, Prof. Cross, of Boston, has made direct measurements of the strengths of the currents generated in the secondary wire of a transmitter induction coil by the variations in the primary coils, and has been thereby able to compare the power of different transmitters, a matter difficult to do when judging by the ear alone.

Three instruments—Edison's, Blake's, and Hunnings'— were thus tested, an organ-pipe sounding under an equal pressure of wind acting on the transmitters at equal distances.

The strengths of the currents registered were as follows:—Edison, ·072 milliampere; Blake ·132 m.a.; and Hunnings, ·556 m.a. This shows a marked superiority in the case of the Hunnings which bears out practical experience.

Experiments were also made by sounding the different vowel sounds, the results coming out in about the same proportion as above. It would be interesting to have other transmitters tested in this manner.

Transmitter Induction Coils.—Experiments made by M. Abrezol, of Geneva, on lines of varying length, to determine the best dimensions to be given to induction coils in order to obtain the best effects, resulted in the recommendation of a coil of the following dimensions:— Primary wire, 180 turns of wire 24 mils dia. (23 gauge), giving a resistance = ·5 ohms. Secondary wire 4,200 turns of wire 6 mils dia., giving a resistance = 250 ohms. Experiments made by Mr. Preece resulted in corroborating the above figures.

CHAPTER VI.

SIGNALLING APPARATUS.

ALTHOUGH signalling between telephone stations has been accomplished by means of the telephone itself, as mentioned on page 57, the universal practice at present is to use some form of *electric bell*, operated either by a battery or by electricity generated mechanically by magneto machines.

The signalling and switching apparatus thus required led to the adoption of what are called *switch-bells*, in which the above apparatus is compactly arranged, and the necessary switching is managed by the aid of an *automatic switch*, which consists of a pivoted lever so arranged that the mere hanging of the receiver on one end of it, when a conversation is finished, changes the connection from the telephone apparatus on to the signalling device and disconnects the transmitter battery circuit, so as to prevent the battery working to waste.

The automatic switch was patented in America, but not in this country, so that its use here is free.

Electric Bells.—As these are much used in telephony, a short description is desirable. The term electric bells is generally applied to those bells which are actuated by batteries, those operated by magneto induction currents being called *magneto bells*. The latter will be described further on in this chapter.

Electric bells are of two kinds, *single stroke* and *trembler*. The former are the simpler, and consist of an electro-magnet, the armature of which has a hammer attached, which strikes on a gong each time a battery is connected to its terminals. The *trembler* bell has, in addition, an arrangement which automatically breaks the circuit when the armature is attracted. Fig. 59 shows a common and reliable form :—
A and B are two terminals ;

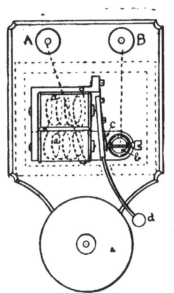

Fig. 59.—Scale ⅓.

A is connected to one end of the magnet coils *a a*, the other end being soldered to the iron frame ; B is connected to pillar *b*, which is insulated from the frame by an ebonite bush. Attached to the armature is a spring, *c*, which in its normal position presses against a contact screw in the top of *b*, which contact forms part of the circuit. On sending a current through the coils the armature is attracted, and the spring *c* leaves the contact screw and breaks the circuit. The armature then falls back and again makes contact, and is again attracted, thus giving rise to repeated strokes of the hammer *d* on the gong *e*, as long as the outside circuit is complete to a battery.

The contact should be platinised, or bad connection will ensue, owing to the sparking. Other practical points are the same as those given for electro-magnets in Chapter I.

The Silvertown Switch-Bell.—Fig. 60 is probably the most common form of switch-bell employed in this country. The connections to the different parts, as shown by the dotted lines, are made by covered wires run in grooves cut in the wooden base of the instrument, which are afterwards filled up with paraffin wax to protect from damp.

Tracing the connection from terminal L, to which the line wire is attached, it passes to *a*, the pivot of the automatic-switch lever *b*, one end of which is formed into a hook, on which the receiver is hung when not in use, and by its weight brings the lever into contact with stud *c*. From *c* connection is made to spring of ringing-key *d* (shown in dotted lines and in side view in Fig. 61), which normally presses against contact plate *e*, but by means of a press-button, *f*, may be pressed against the contact plate *g*. Plate *e* is connected to contact screw *h* of the electric-bell, through the coils of which, *i i*, the connection passes to the terminal E, connected to earth by a wire joined on to a water-pipe.

By the circuit just traced signals may be received

from the instrument at the other end of the line, or by
pressing on the button *f,* spring *e* will be brought into
contact with *g,* which is connected by way of terminal
c to the carbon end of a battery, the zinc end of which
is joined to earth. A current will then pass by spring

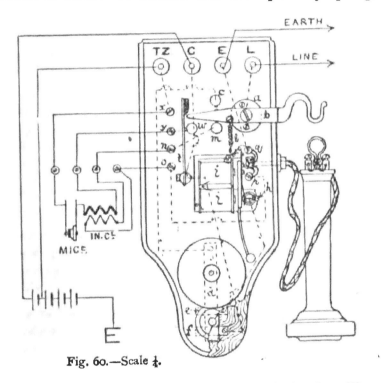

Fig. 60.—Scale ¼.

d, stud *c,* lever *b* and *a* to line, and through the signalling
apparatus at the other end and back by way of earth to
the battery.

On removing the receiver, lever *b* is pulled down by
the spiral spring *l,* into contact with stud *m,* which is
connected to small terminal *n.* From *n,* and a similar

terminal *o* below, connecting wires are run to the secondary of the transmitter induction coil, as shown. From *o* connection is made to terminal *p*, to which, and to the adjoining one, *q*, the ends of the flexible cord of the receiver *r* are attached, *q* being also connected to earth through terminal E, thus completing the connection for speaking.

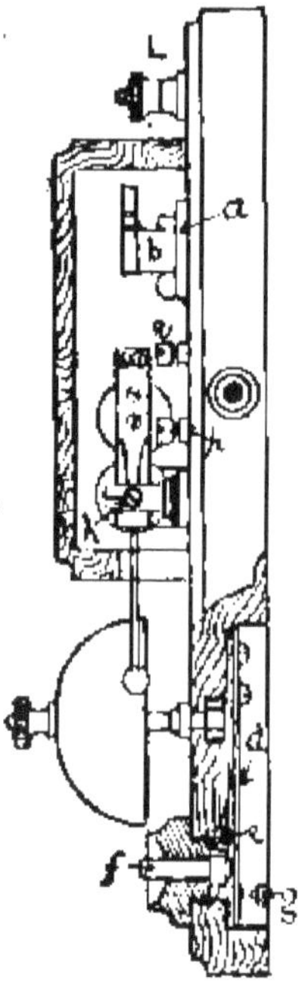

It remains to show how the transmitter battery is disconnected when not required. For lines of $1\frac{1}{2}$ miles or less, the full battery usually consists of four Leclanché cells connected in series. A wire from the first carbon connects to terminal C, and one from the second carbon to terminal T Z, so that the first cell of the battery is included between T Z and C. Starting from T Z, the connection in the bell goes to the small terminal *x*, from which, and terminal *y*, wires are run to the primary wire terminals of the microphone.

Fig. 61.—Scale $\frac{1}{4}$.

From *y* the connection goes to stud *w*, against which, when the receiver is off the hook, spring *t* presses ; *t* is connected to terminal C, the local primary circuit of the microphone being thus completed. On hanging up the receiver the end of lever *b* presses against the bevelled surface of a small block of ebonite fixed in the end of spring *t*, pressing the latter from its contact with *w*, and thus severing the local circuit.

The connections have been so fully traced because the Silvertown may be taken as the type of nearly all switch-bells used for battery signalling, other kinds differing from it only in form or minor details.

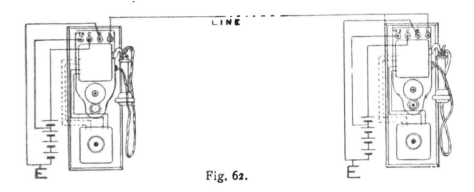

Fig. 62.

Fig. 62 shows two instruments connected up to a line, and forming a complete private installation.

Liverpool Switch-bell, Fig. 63.—A large number of this pattern have been used in London and Lancashire. The lettering of the different parts has been made to correspond with that of the Silvertown, so that the connections may be easily traced.

The principal difference is in the automatic switch, which is made up of a round brass disc, pivoted at its centre, having an ivory projecting pin, which presses against the local battery spring, and breaks the circuit when the receiver is on the hook. Projecting platinum pins in the disc make the bell and telephone contacts by pressing against springs attached to the studs *c* and *m*. Hanging the receiver on the hook causes the disc to revolve a certain distance against the tension of the spiral spring l, and to complete the bell connection. The whole is made in the form of a hinged case, in the

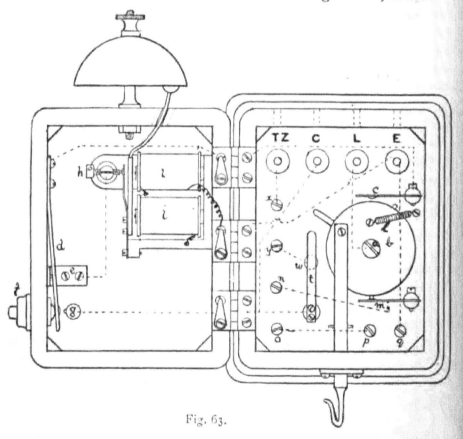

Fig. 63.

front part of which is fixed the electric bell and signalling press-button.

The Silvertown pattern is found more convenient and reliable than the Liverpool. The hook of the latter being small, and below the instrument, is troublesome to use, and its electric bell hammer having an awkward bend in it, it is rather apt to get out of order. The Liverpool has the advantage that all its parts are readily accessible for repairs, etc., while the press button spring of the S.P. is difficult to get at. Being the same

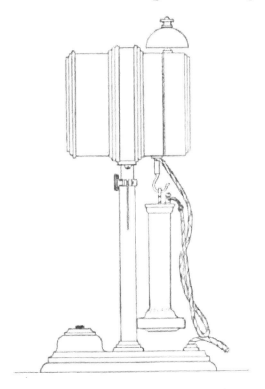

Fig. 64.—Scale ⅓.

size as a Blake transmitter, the L.P. readily lends itself for the construction of a portable desk telephone set, such as shown in Fig. 64, flexible conducting wires being used to join up the battery line, etc.

All contacts of switch-bells should be made with platinum wire let into the ends of screws, studs, etc. This is especially important where any sparking occurs, such as the local battery contact and ringing key. Sometimes silver wire is used for the purpose, but it is poor economy.　The contact between the automatic

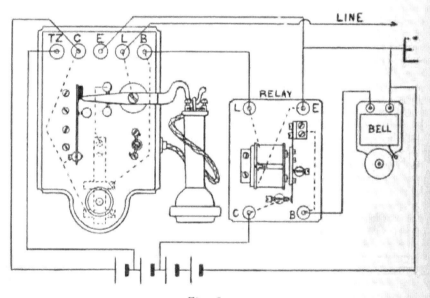

Fig. 65.

switch lever and its pivot should be bridged over with a fine spiral of copper wire, to ensure good contact.

Relays.—When a telephone line worked by battery is above a certain length, say above three or four miles, it becomes desirable to use what is called a *relay* in connection with the instrument.　The object of the relay is to save battery power, by enabling a battery to ring the instrument bell at its own station, the relay itself being operated by a comparatively weak current.

The simplest form is an electro-magnet wound with rather fine wire, with an armature delicately balanced, so that a comparatively weak current will cause it to be attracted. When this happens the armature, or a spring attached to it, makes contact with an insulated pin which closes a circuit, including a battery and instrument bell.

When a relay is used, the instrument bell is usually cut out of the line circuit, and the coils of the relay are joined up in its place. The instrument bell, or, better, a low resistance bell, is then included in the relay contact circuit with a battery of two or three cells, as is shown in Fig. 65. Fig. 66 shows a delicate form of relay, called the Post Office pattern.

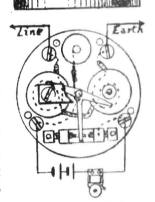

Fig. 66.—Scale ½.

The coils of battery switch-bells are usually wound with wire of 13 mils dia. to a resistance of about 30 ohms. Relay coils to 100 or 200 ohms.

Magneto Switch-Bells.— In the early days of the telephone batteries were almost exclusively used for signalling purposes, but they have now generally given way to mechanical generators of electricity, based on Faraday's discovery that currents can be generated by the movements of coils of wire in the vicinity of magnets. The *magneto switch-bells* have the advantage that they are more self-contained than the battery arrangements, and that they will operate through lines of very high resistance, which would require very strong batteries and relays to work by battery.

Magneto switch-bells consist of four principal parts :—

1. The *magneto-generator*, with its driving gear, by means of which the signalling currents are produced.

2. The *automatic cut-out*, an arrangement for short-circuiting the generator coils when the generator is not being used.

3. The *polarised bell*, which is operated by the currents produced by a magneto generator.

4. The *automatic switch*, which serves the same purpose as those already described in connection with battery switch-bells.

The *magneto-generator*, or simply the *generator*, usually follows the form of a machine first constructed in 1858 by Dr. Werner Siemens, in which a cylindrical armature which he had just previously invented was employed, being caused to revolve between the poles of a powerful horse-shoe magnet.

Figs. 67 and 68 show the magnets of a common form of generator fitted on to cast-iron *pole-pieces*. The pole-pieces are braced together by four brass rods, only two of which, C and D, are shown. The whole is next bored out so as just to allow the Siemens' armature (which is generally about $1\frac{1}{2}$ inches diameter) to revolve freely within. Three horse-shoe

magnets are clamped by iron plates and screws
to the pole-pieces A and B, so that all their marked
ends are on one side. The screws shown at the bottom
are for clamping the generator to the bottom of the
containing case.

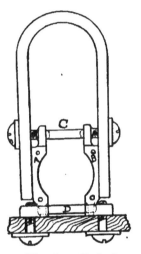

Fig. 67.—Scale ⅛.

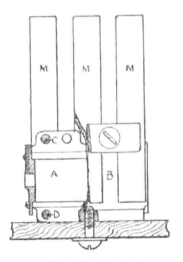

Fig. 68.—Scale ⅛.

The armature for the machine is made by winding
silk-covered copper wire of about 5 mils diameter on a
soft iron core of the shape shown in plan in Fig. 69 and
in end view in Fig. 70, being a cylinder of iron, out of
which has been cut two deep and wide slots, one on each
side, leaving only a comparatively thin web and a pivot
in the centre, on which it may be made to revolve. As
shown in Fig. 69, the web is cut away at each end to
allow for the wire, which is wound on longitudinally in
the recesses thus formed, the surface of the recesses
having been first covered with varnished paper to prevent

accidental contacts.   The wire being wound on until the
armature is nearly filled to the circular form, one end is
connected to a small pin, A, Fig. 69, screwed or driven
into the metal, and the other end to a
pin, B, which is insulated by being im-
bedded in a small ebonite tube, but
makes connection with another brass
pin, C, also insulated by a vulcanite tube
let into the centre of the pivot.

Brass end pieces are attached by
screws to the ends of the magnet pole-
pieces, having bushes in their centre, in

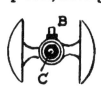

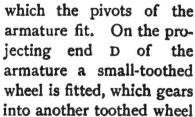

which the pivots of the
armature fit.   On the projecting end D of the
armature a small-toothed
wheel is fitted, which gears
into another toothed wheel

Fig. 69.—Scale ½.   Fig. 70.

about four times its diameter, carried on a shaft which
works in bearings connected to the brass end pieces of
the *armature box*.   This shaft is driven by a crank handle,
brought outside the instrument case, the armature
making four revolutions for each one of the crank.

Mode of Action.—The space between the pole-pieces
of the magnets is a powerful magnetic field, in which
the lines of force go across almost in straight lines
from one pole to the other.   The coil of wire, in revolving in this field, is continually varying the number of
lines of force which pass through it, the number passing
through being greatest when the web of the iron core is

in a position straight across from pole to pole, and least when it is in a position at right angles to this. The direction in which the lines of force pass through the coil alternates with each half revolution, and therefore a complete revolution gives rise to two currents, alternating in direction, if the circuit through the coils is completed.

Another, and perhaps simpler, explanation of the action will be understood by noting the fact that the core of the armature is induced into a magnet by the lines of force passing through it, and that its polarity is reversed twice in every revolution, each of the reversals inducing a current in the surrounding coil, which is opposite in direction to that produced by the previous reversal.

The faster the armature is revolved, the greater the speed of the changes which take place, and the greater is the E.M.F. induced, which is also increased in proportion to the number of turns of wire on the armature, the strength of the magnets, and the softness or *permeability* of the iron of which the core is made.

Driving Gear.—Toothed - wheel gearing is now usually employed for revolving the generator armature. The teeth of the wheels must be fine and accurately cut by machinery, otherwise they make a disagreeable noise when worked. It was this noise which prevented toothed gearing coming into general use sooner, many people preferring the usually quiet methods of driving by friction gear or india-rubber bands and grooved pulleys.

Automatic Cut-out.—When the generator is not

actually in use for ringing, it is important that its resistance, which is considerable, should be cut out of the circuit, since it is useless, and would weaken the received signals on the bells. In order to effect this purpose many ingenious devices have been invented which are called *automatic cut-outs.* In most cases the force required to turn the armature is utilized to cause the removal of a short circuit of the armature coil, and thus throw its wire into the circuit.

Perhaps the most novel and interesting plan is that adopted in the Post pattern magneto-bell, in which centrifugal force is made to effect the object. Fig. 71

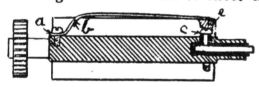

Fig. 71.—Scale ¼.

is a section through the pivot of the armature core of this bell. At the point *a*, where one end of its coil is connected, a spring, *b*, is clamped, having attached at its opposite end a small brass block, *e*, which presses against the insulated pin *c*, to which the other end of the coil is attached, as in Fig. 69. Directly the armature is revolved, block *e* flies out, and the short-circuit of the coil, which previously existed, is broken, and remains so as long as the revolution continues ; *e* and *b* are prevented from flying out too far by a loop attached to *e*, which passes round the axle.

The *cut-out* adopted in the Western Electric Company's magneto-bells is shown in Fig. 72. The driving shaft A runs in bearings, C and D, attached to the end pieces of the armature box. E is a toothed-wheel

gearing into a smaller one attached to the armature.
E is driven by a steel pin driven through the shaft
bearing against the inclined face of a V-shaped recess
cut in its boss, F.   On attempting to turn the crank B,
some force is necessary before the armature can be
moved, and the result of applying this force is that
the pin G moves up the inclined face of the recess,
withdrawing the end of the shaft from the spring J,
against which it is usually pressed by the spiral spring
H.   The spring J also presses against the insulated

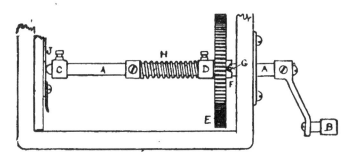

Fig. 72.—Scale ⅓.

pin at the end of the armature pivot, to which one end
of the coil is attached, and as the other end of the
coil is attached to the framework, through the pivots,
it is plain that when the shaft A touches J the coils
will be short-circuited, and, when drawn away by the
act of driving, this short circuit will be broken.

The Polarised Bell.—As the currents which work this,
produced by a generator, follow each other with great
rapidity (each turn of the handle generating eight
separate currents, and being turned on an average about
four times each second, thus producing thirty-two

separate currents per second), it follows that the bell must be very sensitive to respond to each of these pulsations.   The speed of turning the handle of the generator also varies greatly with different persons, so that the bell must be able to respond equally well to varying speeds.   An ordinary battery bell will only respond satisfactorily to currents following each other at a certain rate, and will therefore not be suitable for magneto-generated currents.   It has been known for a long period in telegraphy that the instruments which respond best to rapid pulsations of currents are those which are polarized, that is to say, in which the moving parts are magnetic in themselves, or are maintained in a magnetic state by the induction of magnets.   The well-known Siemens' relay is constructed on this principle, and a modification of it was adopted to form the polarized bell.

Figs. 73 and 74 represent a common form of the bell.   An electro-magnet is formed of bobbins, A and B (wound to about a resistance of 100 ohms each), screwed to a soft-iron base, C, serving as its yoke.   In the centre of C is screwed one pole, N, of a permanent magnet.   At the ends of the base C two brass rods, E and F, are screwed, the prolongation of the screws serving to clamp the bell to the instrument case G.   E and F are also furnished with screws and nuts at their opposite ends, with which the brass bar H is secured in position, and can be adjusted.   In the centre of H a pivot is formed, in which a soft-iron armature, J, can vibrate about its centre, just in front of the ends of the magnet cores, in which brass pins are fitted to prevent magnetic contact. The hammer and rod, K, is attached to one side of the armature, and moves with it, striking alternately on the gongs L and M fixed outside on the front of the case G.

The S pole of the magnet comes over the centre of the armature J, and polarises it by induction, the middle being made of north polarity, and the ends of south polarity, whilst the ends of the cores are made of north polarity by the N pole of the magnet.

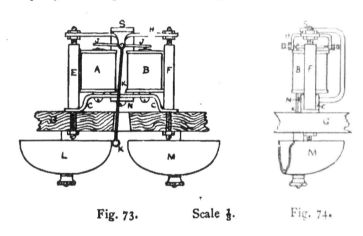

Fig. 73.   Scale ⅛.   Fig. 74.

Action.—The effect of passing a current through the coils is to strengthen the north polarity of one core, and to weaken or altogether neutralise the north polarity of the other core, the effect being that the armature is strongly attracted to one core and not at all by the other. The next reversal of current causes the core which was strengthened before to be weakened, and *vice versâ*, so that the armature vibrates over to the opposite core, and in doing so causes the hammer to strike on the gongs, and so on repeatedly.

Sometimes two polarising magnets are used, one to each core, but the action and effect are similar.

Automatic Switch.—This differs but little from that used on battery switch-bells in regard to principle, but each maker adopts a different pattern. There is, however, one point in which it differs from those described, which is that the local battery contact is made on the metal of the lever itself, there being no necessity to insulate it from the lever as with battery switch-bells, where the transmitter cell forms part of the ringing battery, which has its zinc pole permanently connected to earth, so that if the local contact were made on the lever a current would pass to line whenever the instrument was used for speaking. This will not occur with a magneto bell, with which the transmitter battery is the only one used, and is not connected to earth.

A very common and satisfactory form of switch is shown in Figs. 75 and 76:—A A is a piece of ebonite on which the pivot brass piece D is mounted, the pronged lever B being pivoted at C. Attached at right angles to B is a wedge-shaped brass piece, *e e*, which, when the receiver is off the lever, makes contact with the three springs, *a b c*, being drawn up against them by the tension of the spiral spring *f*. Line being connected to the lever, and spring *c* to the telephone instruments, the circuit will be complete for speaking, the local battery circuit being completed through the springs *a* and *b*, and the portion of the lever against which they press.

On hanging the receiver on the prong the lever is depressed and brought into contact with spring *d*, which is connected to the generator and polarised bell, the other end of these being to earth, as shown in Fig. 82. The spring *g* (Fig. 76), to which a connection is made from the line terminal, presses continually on the top of

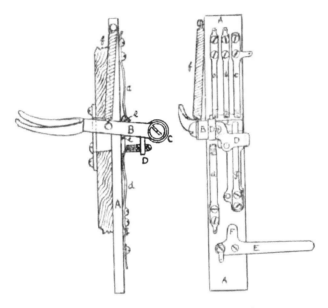

Fig. 75.   Scale ½.   Fig. 76.

e, and ensures a good contact. The spring E presses on the insulated pin at the end of the generator-armatures and the automatic shunt of its coils is made and broken at the point F.

A switch which has been recently introduced by the Western Electric Company is shown in Figs. 77 and 78, and has some rather novel features. Corresponding parts are lettered similarly to Fig. 75. The strong spring *d* serves both as the bell contact spring and in place of the spiral spring for throwing up the lever when the receiver is removed, its end bearing on a button of ebonite, *w*, on the lever when the latter is up, and on a metal piece, *x*, when the lever is down. Similarly the ends of the three springs *a b c*, shown separately in Fig. 78, press on the ebonite piece *y* when the lever is down, and on the contact plate *s* when the lever is up, all the springs changing contact by a kind of

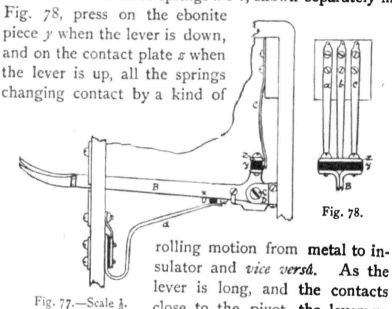

Fig. 78.

Fig. 77.—Scale ⅓.

rolling motion from metal to insulator and *vice versâ*. As the lever is long, and the contacts close to the pivot, the leverage is great, and the springs can be made strong and the contacts firm.

It would seem to be desirable that hooks should take the place of prongs, as the original form of Bell receiver for which they were designed is rapidly giving way to other forms, for which the prongs are not suitable.

Lightning Arrestors.—As the bell and armature coils

of a magneto bell are of fine wire and high resistance
(the former being about 200 ohms and the latter 400 or
500 ohms) they are especially liable to damage by
lightning, and should therefore be provided with some
form of lightning discharger
or protector. By far the most
common form is one in which
a plate with saw teeth is
clamped close to, but not
touching, one or two other
plates, the terminal screws of
the instrument being usually
attached to these plates, as

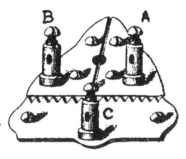

Fig. 79.

shown in Figs. 79 and 80, which show two of the most
common forms. The third intermediate terminal is
furnished in case the instrument is used as an intermediate one on a line of three or more stations, or on a

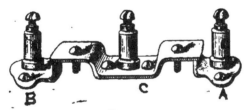

Fig. 80

metallic circuit line, the earth being then only connected to C. If it is used for a terminal station, B and C
are both connected to earth, and A to the line wire.
Fig. 80 protector is adjusted by screwing down the pins
shown. To give the best protection the saw teeth
should be milled sharp, and adjusted very close, when

a charge of high potential electricity will spark across the space, instead of going through the coils of the instrument, and perhaps fusing them. It is not advisable to adjust too closely, as they are apt to short-circuit the instrument, by getting together, through the warping of the timber, etc.

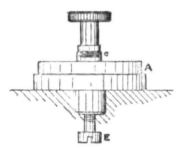

Fig. 81.

Fig. 81 shows a form of protector used by the British Post Office, which consists of two metal discs kept apart by a thin disc of mica, having three perforations. The terminal passes through both brass discs, but is insulated from the upper one by the ebonite collar *e*. The earth connection is made to terminal E, and line to disc A. Fig. 81 is two-thirds full size.

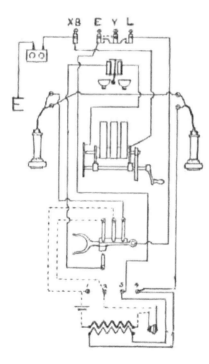

Fig. 82.

Connections. — Fig. 82 shows how the various parts of a magneto switch-bell are connected together. Terminals are shown on the right for an extra receiver. If one is not used, these terminals must be joined together by a piece of thick wire. Four terminals are shown at the top; three, L, E, and Y, are the ordinary ones just described, and X B is provided so that an *extension bell* (which is merely a polarised bell in a case by itself, so that it may be fixed away from the telephone instrument) may be connected in the manner shown, so that it may not be included in the speaking circuit. If an extra bell is not required, X B and E must be looped together by a short piece of wire. The rest of the sketch will, it is hoped, explain itself.

Fig. 83 shows a Western Electric Company's magneto switch-bell, complete, with Blake transmitter and box for transmitter cell fitted on a backboard. The top of the

Fig. 83.

cell box forms a small writing-desk. Fig. 84 gives a general view of the internal arrangement of a similar switch-bell, on the door of which is fitted a Blake transmitter.

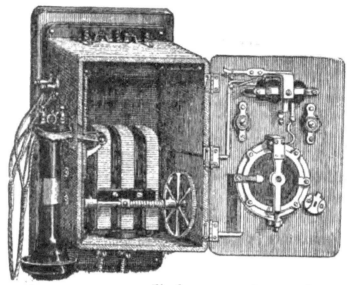

Fig. 84.

Fig. 85 shows a useful form of movable desk magneto set, made by the Consolidated Telephone Company.

Carty's Magneto-Bell.— Fig. 86 gives the connections of this instrument, which has been lately introduced in America, and appears likely to replace the ordinary arrangement.

The novelty consists, not in the construction, but in the connections of

Fig. 85.

the different parts. The generator and bell, instead of being joined in series in the same circuit, are connected in multiple circuit, the bell being also joined permanently to line between the L and E terminals of the instrument.

Instead of an automatic *cut-out*, an automatic *cut-in* is used to join the generator coil to line when in action,

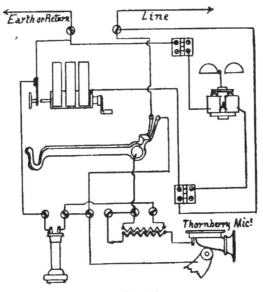

Fig. 86.

this coil being disconnected when not in use. No lower contact to the automatic lever is necessary.

As many as twenty or thirty stations provided with these bells may be joined up on one line, and will ring and speak well, whilst not more than five or six can be satisfactorily worked with the ordinary magneto, joined up in series.

Comparison of Battery and Magneto Systems.— Experience with both systems of working has shown that for short lines of one or two miles in length the battery system is most economical; but the reverse is the case for long lines, because larger batteries and relays have to be used for battery signalling, which add to the cost and complication.

For simplicity the magneto has a great advantage, as it requires no addition, whatever length of line it has to work through (a good magneto being able to ring through 12,000 ohms' resistance), and only two wires have usually to be run in connecting it up, as compared with the four or five required for battery systems.

The magneto does not lend itself readily, however, to special arrangements for ringing off and signalling, and the noise and trouble of working is sometimes complained of by subscribers.

The chief item of maintenance in both systems is in connection with the transmitter cells, which require to be inspected at least every four months. Ringing batteries have comparatively little work to do, and their cost of maintenance is but small. Large-sized cells should be used for the transmitters, as, containing more working material, they are not so soon exhausted.

Instrument Fixing.—Many practical points need to be attended to in fixing or fitting up the instruments, a few of which will be briefly mentioned.

Position of Instruments.—A position should be chosen which will be as quiet as possible, on a solid wall, not

subject to vibration, and on which a good light falls.
Care should also be taken that room is left for the user
to hold up the receiver to his ear without his arm
coming into contact with a side wall or other object.
The height should be regulated so that the transmitter
funnel will be on a level with the mouth of the shortest
person who has to use it, as it is easy for a tall person
to stoop, but very inconvenient for a short person to
stretch up. In speaking, the face is naturally directed
downwards.

If the above conditions cannot be obtained, and a
noisy position has to be chosen, a second receiver should
be used to exclude the noise, or a silent cabinet constructed, in which to place the instrument. If the wall
vibrates it will give rise to noise in the transmitter
unless the latter is isolated by being suspended on
flexible springs, preferably of india-rubber.

Having marked the position of the fixing screws
(inquiry having previously been made as to the position
of buried gas-pipes), round plug-holes are made in the
wall, and round or octagonal-sectioned wooden plugs,
of about 3 inches in length, tightly driven in. To these
the backboard of the instrument is firmly screwed. The
instrument should have been previously set up and
thoroughly tested before leaving the workshop or test-
room.

The wires are next connected up to the proper
terminals, copper wire, braided with cotton and paraffined,
and of about No. 18 gauge, or 49 mils diameter, being
used, if the room in which they are fixed is thoroughly

dry.   If this is at all doubtful, gutta-percha (or G.P., as
it is commonly termed) covered wire, with an outer
covering of cotton, should be used, the cotton covering
preventing the G.P. from crumbling and falling away
from the wire, which it is apt to do after a time.

In stapling the wires care must be taken that the
covering is not damaged.   Tinned steel staples of a
U shape and about ⅝ inch in length are used.   If more
than one wire is secured under the same staple, which is
seldom advisable, special precautions, such as putting
a slip of leather under the staples, should be taken
to prevent damage.   Care should be taken that
staples used for adjacent wires should not come into
contact.

If a battery is used, a cool place somewhere out of
sight should be chosen for it, a cellar being often
selected.

All joints in the wires must be soldered.   This is best
done by using resin as a flux ; but a very good soldering
solution, suitable for all soldering purposes, may be
made up of the following ingredients :—1 pint of
methylated spirits, 2 ozs. of glycerine, and 3 ozs. of
chloride of zinc.

The earth connection for the instrument should be
made with a thick copper wire, well soldered on to a
main water-pipe.   If such cannot be obtained, an earth
plate of galvanised iron, about two feet square, should
be buried in damp ground, and the earth wire connected.

Tools Required.—The tools necessary for fixing are:
Cutting pliers, large and small screw-drivers, gimlets,

bradawls, plugging chisel, large and small hammer, 2-foot rule, bell-hanger's augur, tenon saw, and soldering iron.

In addition to above, a joiner's chisel, detector galvanometer, and a pair of tweezers will often prove useful. The plugging chisel should be 9 or 10 inches

Fig. 87.

long, and be provided with a cutting edge, somewhat of the shape of a metal drill (Fig. 87). It is advisable that the small tools should be mounted on a slip of leather, such as used by joiners. This can be rolled up, and will protect the tools, and a glance will show whether all the tools are collected.

I

CHAPTER VII.

INTERMEDIATE SWITCHES AND SWITCH-BOARDS.

THE simplest form of a telephone installation is a single-line wire connected to a telephone set at each end. Next to this in simplicity is the arrangement in which one instrument serves two lines, each having a telephone set at the other end, or, in other words, when

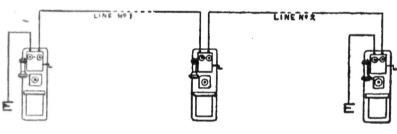

Fig. 88.

there are three instruments connected to one line, one being intermediate to the other two. Such an arrangement may be worked without the addition of special apparatus, either by connecting the intermediate station apparatus directly in the line circuit, without an earth connection, as shown in Fig. 88, or, which is the more satisfactory plan, by connecting the intermediate

instrument as a shunt to the line running direct between
the end stations, as shown in Fig. 89. The objections
to both these plans are that no privacy can be observed,
as ringing and speaking are common to all the stations,
and a code of signals is necessary for ringing, to inti-
mate which station is required. The first plan has the
further disadvantage that the bell coils will have to be
spoken through, which is very injurious to the speaking.
More than three instruments may be joined up to a line
on either of these plans, and such arrangements are

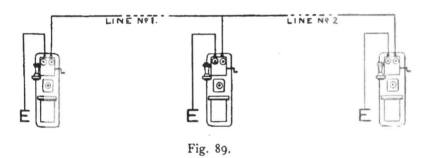

Fig. 89.

preferred by many firms, and have given satisfaction,
especially the shunt plan, by which a large number of
instruments may be worked on one line.

Intermediate switches are, however, much oftener
used for the working of three stations on one line.
What is required with these is that the intermediate
station, where the switch is fixed, shall be enabled to
get into connection with either of the end stations, and
while so switched on to one, the other station shall be
able to signal. The two end stations must be able to
speak together, without their conversation being in

danger of being overheard at the intermediate station, but so that they can signal the latter when required.

Fig. 90 shows a form of switch, many of which are now in use, devised by the writer in 1880 to satisfy these requirements. Five terminals, marked IN, L_1, B_2, L_2, and E, are arranged in a row at the upper part of the instrument. Clamped under the three centre

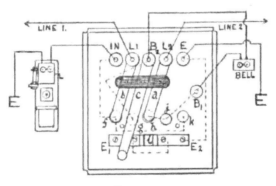

Fig. 90.

terminals, and held by lock nuts, are three springs, b c and d, c being longer and furnished with a handle knob. The springs are joined together with an ebonite bar, e, so that they all move together. The ends of b and d can make contact on to the brass studs f g h j and k, and the handle bar on to the earth plates E E, except when in its middle position, when it is insulated on the piece of ebonite i. The two lines are connected to the terminals L_1 and L_2.

Tracing the connection (which is given in dotted lines) from L_1 when the handle is on the left-hand side, as shown, it goes by spring b and stud f to terminal

IN, to which is connected the line terminal of the telephone set. Speaking and ringing can therefore go on with the station connected to No. 1 line. From L_2 the connection is by spring d to stud h, thence to stud j and terminal B, through an extension bell, as

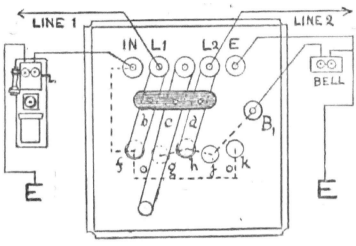

Fig. 91.—Scale ½.

shown, to terminal B_2, handle bar c, to earth - plate E, so that signals can therefore be sent from the end station on line No. 2.

On moving the handle over from left to right the line connections will be reversed, No. 2 line being then connected to the telephone set, and No. 1 line to the extension bell.

On putting the handle in the central position the telephone set will be altogether cut out, and the end stations will be connected directly to each other, with the extension bell attached to the switch included in the circuit, in order to signal the intermediate station when finished.

By arranging that the extension bell shall be connected as a shunt to earth when the end stations are through to each other, the connections of the switch 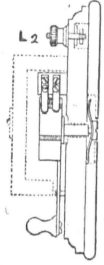 may be much simplified, as shown in Fig. 91. This is also a more satisfactory plan of working, as the coils of the bell have not to be spoken through.

Of course, more than three stations on a line may be worked by providing each of the intermediate ones with a similar switch. The second plan of working is then much the more satisfactory.

Miller's Intermediate Switch.—This is a very neat and reliable instrument, designed for the same purpose as above by Mr. Miller, of Dundee. Figs. 92 and 93 are views of the instrument.

Fig. 92.—Scale ⅓.

to a scale of one-third, and Fig. 94 a diagrammatic representation of its connections. Six terminals, L_1, B_1, B_2, L_2, IN, and E are provided, and six german silver springs connected to the terminals are arranged to bear on brass segments fastened to the outside surface of an ebonite cylinder, *a*, provided with a handle, *b*. The figures show the divisions between the segments, and how some of them are connected together. It will be seen that the top segment is sub-divided in its width. Four of the springs are clamped to the ebonite block *c*.

In the position shown the end stations are through to each with the extra or extension bell intermediate. On turning the handle to the *right* No. 1 line will be connected to the telephone set, and No. 2 line to the extra bell, and *vice versâ* when the handle is turned to the *left.*

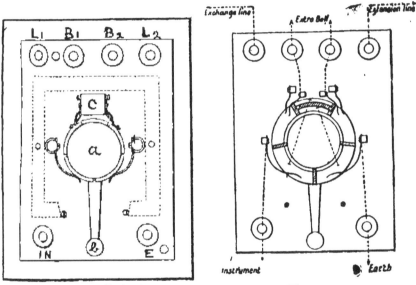

Fig. 93.—Scale ⅜.   Fig. 94.

Different toned bells and gongs should be provided in connection with these intermediate switches, so that there may be no difficulty in deciding which of the two bells, the instrument or the extension, has rung at any time, otherwise much trouble may be occasioned.

When through connection between the end stations is not required or desirable, the connections of the switches above described are so altered that there is no circuit through when the handle is in the centre, or a simpler form of switch may be used, such as shown in Fig. 95. This is called a *double-bar* switch. The connections will be understood from the sketch.

It frequently happens that subscribers leave the office in which their telephone is fixed, and when they return wish to know if the bell or bells have been rung in their

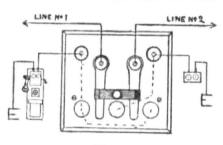

Fig. 95.

absence. In such cases an indicating disc may be attached to the bell, in such ·a manner that the bell hammer in moving shall release a catch, and allow the disc to fall into view.

Such arrangements are, however, liable to produce faults, and it is a better plan to have recourse to *drop indicators* connected up in place of the bell coils. A bell and battery may be connected up with these so that as long as the shutter of the indicator is down the bell will continue to ring, but a *two-way switch* should be provided in the circuit of the bell in order to prevent it ringing at night or when not desirable.

Two-way switches are often required for the purpose of breaking a circuit or to change on to different apparatus. Figs. 96, 97 and 98 show a good form. The handle is attached to the centre of a brass spring A A, one end of which bears on piece B, and the other end on one of the brass pieces C or D, according to the direction in which the handle is turned.

Fig. 99 is a back view of what may be called a perfect two-way switch designed by Mr. A. R. Bennett. The front is similiar to Fig. 96. The comb springs *c* and *d*,

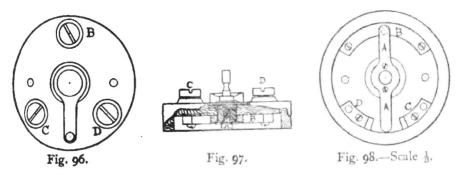

Fig. 96.   Fig. 97.   Fig. 98.—Scale ½.

Fig. 99, are attached to the terminals C and D. Underneath, but not touching *c* and *d*, is a double comb spring, *b b b*, connected to the handle terminal B; and attached to the handle is a double wedge-shaped brass arm, *a a*, which presses between the springs *b* and *c*, or *b* and *d* when the handle is put to one side or the other, thus ensuring a double means of contact, one from the handle direct by arm *a*, and another from comb *b* through arm *a*.

Fig. 99.—Scale ½.

Switch-boards.—When more than two lines have to be

served by one telephone instrument, it is usual to employ what is called a *switch-board* in place of a handle-switch and bells, each line being connected to a *drop indicator* provided on the board, and special arrangements made for connecting any pair of lines together. The construction of a handle-switch for, say, four lines, although possible, would be difficult, owing to the large number of connections required to provide for the different combinations.

Before describing the boards themselves it will be advisable to explain the

Drop Indicators or *Annunciators* which are used in connection with them. These usually consist of an

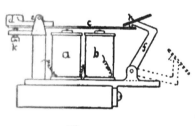

electro-magnet, with an armature so arranged that when it is attracted, a shutter, which was held in position by it, is allowed to fall and expose a number or surface, which will attract attention.

Fig. 100.

Fig. 100 shows an old form. The electro-magnet, *a b*, attracting the soft iron armature *c*, allows the lever *f*, provided with red disc *h*, to fall, the end of *f* being previously hooked in a hole in the end of *c*. *c* is pivoted at *e*, and is provided with a counter weight, *d*, and an adjusting screw, *k*.

The faults of this drop are that too much friction is put on the armature by the weight of the overhanging disc and lever *f*, and that the space between the armature and the core of *a* must be rather large to allow of sufficient catch on the drop, and since the magnetic attraction diminishes very rapidly, as the distance of the armature increases, there will be a loss of power. The best effect will be produced when the attraction is exerted near the pivot of the armature, and the necessary movement of the releasing catch obtained by using a long light lever attached to it. The armature can then be adjusted, comparatively close to the cores, but must be prevented by brass core pins from actually touching when attracted.

The Western Electric Company's drop is constructed on this plan, and has almost superseded all other forms, except those used for special purposes. Fig. 101 gives a side view of one about full size, only one coil of the horse-shoe electro-magnet being seen:— *a* is ❧ the drop shutter pivoted at the bottom ; *b*

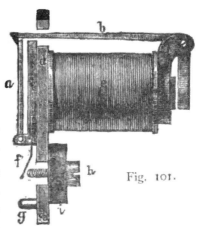

Fig. 101.

a lever attached at right angles to the armature, which is placed very near the cores of the magnet *e*. These cores at the other end are attached by iron screws to the strip of iron, *d d* (shown in section), which forms the yoke and support for some five or ten drop indicators. Along the back of *d d* a strip of ebonite, *i*, is attached, and through this and underneath the centre of each drop a screw, *h*, projects to the front through a hole drilled in *d d*.

On the drop *a* being released, it falls and presses the end of a light german silver spring, *f*, against the end of *h*. One end of a circuit, including a battery and bell, is connected to the strips *d*, and the other end to each of the screws *h* on the board. On *f* (which is clamped to the framework) and *h* therefore coming into contact, the bell is caused to ring by the completion of what is called the *local* or *night-bell* circuit, and continues to ring until the drop is raised. During the day the local circuit is usually disconnected by a two-way switch, as operators are then in attendance at each table, and a falling drop secures instant attention.

The resistance of the W. E. drops is usually about 100 ohms. They are made in three sizes, which differ only in detail.

Some special forms of drops will be described when dealing with switch-room systems.

Small Switch-boards.—Fig. 102 represents a type of switch-board which was designed by the writer in 1881 for the use of private telephonic exchanges, and small public ones. The board shown is intended to accommodate five lines or six stations, including the *central* or switch-board station itself. They have been made in all sizes up 30 lines, a board for the latter number having been in use for about seven years at the Manchester chief fire station.

The line wires are attached to the terminals 1, 2, 3, 4, 5, each of these being connected to a W. E. drop and a switch-handle numbered correspondingly. As shown in the figure, the switch handles are making contact on earth studs underneath. The corresponding pairs of the two sets of four brass bars A B C D are connected together by wires behind the board A to A, B to B, and so on, and on a call being received, say, from No. 2 station for connection to No. 5 station, the two switch-handles 2 and 5 are connected on to one of the four pairs of bars, say A A. The two stations can then converse together. The telephone set in connection with the board is connected to the terminal T, and thence to the switch-handle T for answering the calls, etc. The boards may be connected up in several different ways : — The drops may be connected permanently in the circuits, as described above, or as shunts to earth, or

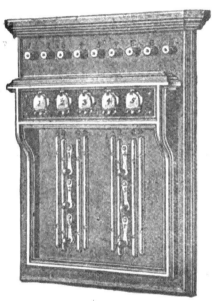

Fig. 102.

they may be cut out altogether when speaking, and separate *ring-off drops* connected to the connecting bars A B C D, as shown in Fig. 103, which is the most satisfactory plan. The terminals B B of Fig. 102 are for the local or night-bell.

A pattern of small switch-board very much used is shown in Fig. 104. W. E. drops are employed, besides

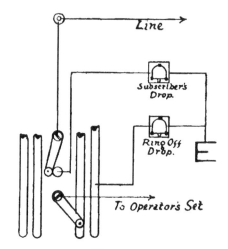

Fig. 103.

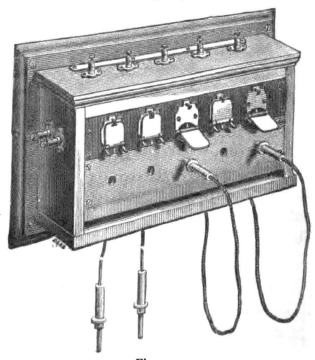

Fig. 104.

which each line is furnished with what is called a *Spring-jack* or *Switch-jack.* Connections are made between the lines by means of round brass plugs carried at the ends of flexible conducting cords.

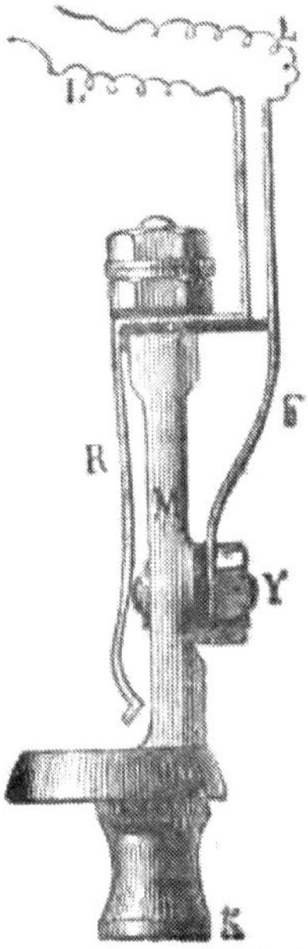

Spring-jacks have now become very important adjuncts to the telephone, and a very large number are in use.

Fig. 105 is a side view of a form much used :—M K is a brass or bronze casting which is turned at the K end, and bored for the insertion of the brass plug shown in Fig. 106. At Y a hole is drilled and bushed with vulcanite through which a pin is inserted and secured by a nut, which also secures a spring connection, F. At the end of M is a screw pin furnished with nuts and washers, which clamp the phosphor bronze spring R in position ; R is insulated from the casting by pieces of vulcanite, and presses strongly on the head of the pin Y. (For use on any switch-boards but the *multiple*, which will be described in the next chapter, it is not necessary to insulate the spring R.) The spring-jacks are fixed in position by inserting the part K in holes bored in the woodwork of the switch-boards, and securing by a screw passing through the projecting flange shown.

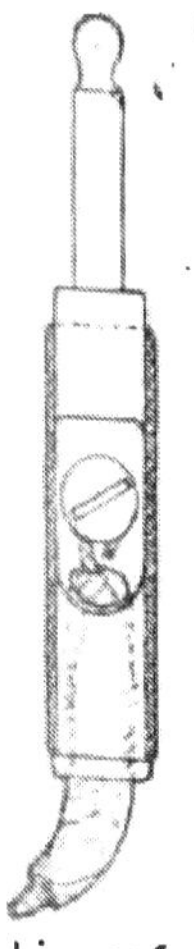

Fig. 105.—Scale ⅔.

Fig. 106. Scale ½.

Referring again to Fig. 104, the lines are connected to

the terminals at the top, from thence to the drops, then to the R springs of the spring-jacks, and through Y to earth, as shown in Fig. 107. The effect of inserting a plug in one of the *jacks* is that the end of the plug lifts the line spring R from pin Y, and thereby connects the line on to the plug and connecting cord. The operating telephone set is provided with a single plug and cord for answering the calls, but the connections between any two lines are made by two plugs on the ends of a

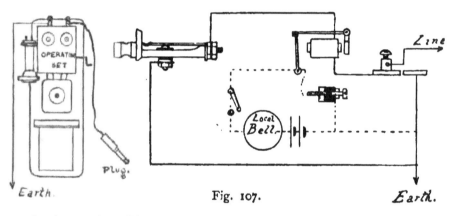

Fig. 107.

single cord. Fig. 104 shows Nos. 2 and 5 lines thus connected, and a spare pair of plugs and cord left.

The above class of boards is only intended to accommodate from 3 to about 25 lines; when a larger number has to be served an *exchange* form of board is used, in which special provision is made for quick operating by special switches, which also provide for the supervision of the lines when in use.

The original method of dealing with a large number of lines in this country was to provide a large board on which the lines were connected to a kind of flat spring-jack. From these connection was normally made to the drops grouped on another part of the board. Operators stood in front of this board, and, by means of cords provided with a brass shoe at each end, connected the lines on to operators sitting at tables arranged in a semi-circle round the large board. The latter operators answered the calls, ascertained the numbers wanted, and called out these to the board operator for connection by means of the shoes and cord, afterwards calling for the subscribers to be disconnected when it had been ascertained that they had finished.

It is evident that this was a cumbrous and slow method of working, and liable to give rise to many mistakes, and so this arrangement soon gave way to what may be called self-contained boards, in which the same operator answered the calls and made the necessary connections. Two or three forms of such boards, which have been in extensive use, will next be described.

Exchange Switch-boards may be divided into two classes: (1) Those based on what is called the *Swiss* commutator principle, in which two sets of metal bars cross each other at right angles, the subscriber's lines being connected to one set. Any two lines may be connected by joining any one of the cross-bars to the two-line bars by some means such as metal plugs passing through and fitting in holes drilled in both sets of bars at their points of crossing. The principle will be understood by reference to Fig. 108, which shows a six-line switch-board. Boards on the Swiss principle

K

were very extensively used a few years back, but have now generally given place to those on (2) the *cord, plug,*

Fig. 108.

and spring-jack system, in which connections are made as already described.

Williams' Slide Switch-board.—This interesting form of board, on the Swiss principle, was much used for exchanges at Glasgow and Manchester, until it was superseded by the multiple board, but is still used in small centres. Fig. 109 is part of a front view of a 50-line board, and Fig. 110 a shortened section. The lines were connected to the top of the brass vertical bars *a a a*, each of which is provided with a brass sliding-piece, *b b b*, a spiral spring on which presses forward the end, which has a V-shaped recess formed in it. Under normal conditions the sliders rest on the heads of the pins *c*, to which is connected one end of the drop indicator coils, the other end of the latter being connected permanently to earth by the bar *d*. Connections are made by placing the sliders of any two subscribers on to any one of the horizontal brass rods 1, 2, 3, 4, 5, about 50 of which are provided on each table. The operator's set

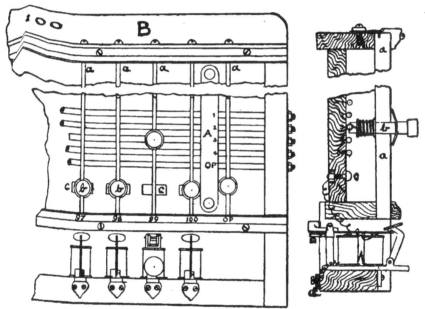

Fig. 109.—Scale ¼.

Fig. 110.—Scale ¼.

is connected to one of the rods, and also to one of the vertical bars o p. Some of the rods are kept for local connections on the one table, and the rest are joined to the other boards in the room for connecting a subscriber on one board to one on another. Ring-off drops are attached to the connecting rods, and form a shunt to earth.

The Gilliland Board is a form which has done good

service. The line and connecting bars are in this board formed of strips of brass bent into peculiar shapes, so as to bring them both to the same surface level. The line strips 1, 2, 3, 4, 5 (Fig. 111) extend from front to back of the table, and are of a crimped form. The connecting strips pass under these at right angles, but

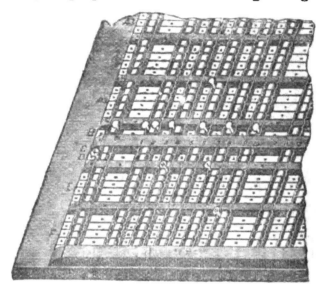

Fig. 111.

are bent so as to project up between each pair of line strips, and connection is made by inserting double connecting springs at these points, as shown at H and I, Nos. 4 and 7 lines being there shown connected. Line strip L is connected to the operator's telephone, and M is connected to generator or battery. Connecting strip B is to earth, and each line is normally plugged on to this. The lines go first through the drop, and then on to the line strip, so that the drops are always in circuit,

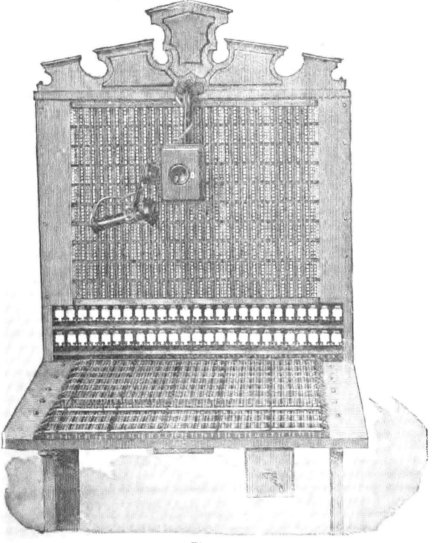

Fig. 112.

and have to be spoken through. Strips C and D are

connected to operator's telephone and ringing generator respectively. The line strips are divided into groups of ten, and the connecting strips into groups of five, some of the latter groups being for connection to other tables, and some for local connections. Fig. 112 gives a general view of a Gilliland 50-line board, fitted with operator's transmitter and receiver fitted on brackets, the receiver being adjustable.

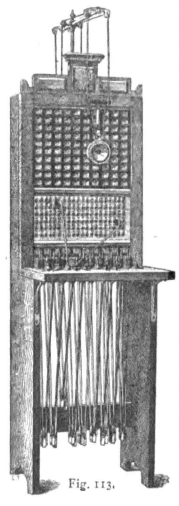

Fig. 113.

Standard Switch-board.— This is a form of plug-and-cord board which is now very much used for small exchanges of up to 400 or 500 lines. It is made by the Western Electric Company. The board shown in Fig. 113 is for 100 lines, and is intended to be worked by one operator. In a busy centre this would entail very heavy work. In such cases it is more usual to employ 50-line boards.

Subscribers' drops of small size are arranged at the top in rows of ten. Below these, in five rows of 20 each, are the spring-jacks

connected to the drops; below these is another row of
20 jacks, which are used for the purpose of transferring
connections to other tables when the
jack of the subscriber wanted is out
of the direct reach of the plugs and
cords used. The latter, 20 in number, are arranged in pairs on a horizontal table, the cords passing
through holes bored in the table, and
kept straight and tidy by weights
and pulleys. The plugs rest in an
upright position on the table, on

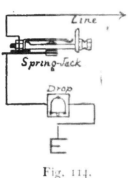

Fig. 114.

which are arranged ten cam switches, for connecting the
operator's telephone to any pair of cords, and ringing keys

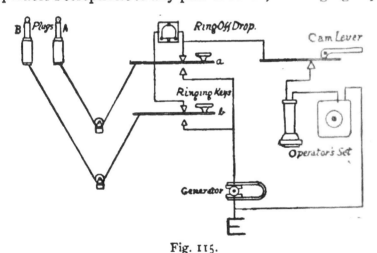

Fig. 115.

for calling the subscribers. Just above the table is fixed
a row of ten ring-off drops, one to each pair of cords.
Fig. 114 shows the connections of one of the lines, and

Fig. 115 of a pair of cords to the ring-off drops and the operator's instruments. Suppose plug A is inserted in the spring-jack, the line connection will be diverted from its drop through the cord and ringing key to the operator's set, if the cam lever is in the position shown. To connect a second line, plug B is inserted in its jack,

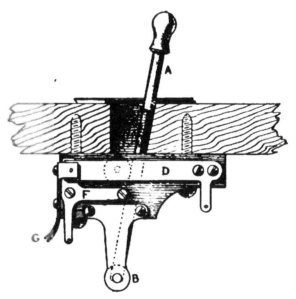

Fig. 116.—Scale ¼.

the ringing key *b* is pressed for a few seconds, bringing the cord and line connected to it into connection with the magneto generator (which is usually driven by power) or a ringing battery. The two lines will then be complete through the ring-off drop, and the operator, after noting that conversation has commenced, cuts out her instrument from the circuit by raising the cam-lever to the upright position. When finished speaking, the subscribers give a turn or two on their magneto, which operates the ring-off drop, and the plugs are withdrawn from the jacks by the operator.

Many improvements have been made in the operator's apparatus used on these tables. Instead of the cam-lever a form of double switch, called the *Dewar Table-key* (Figs. 116 and 117), is now used. It is a kind of

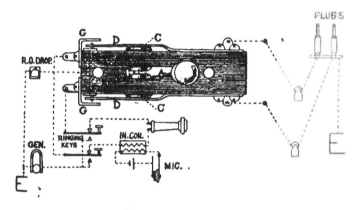

Fig. 117.

double press-button, mounted on a block of ebonite, and operated by pressing the handle-bar A pivoted at B between the two ebonite buttons C C. The effect of this is to press out the two springs D D from contact plates F F to the outer contact plates G G. As shown, D D are connected to the cords and plugs, F F are connected together and to one end of the ring-off drop coils, the other end of the latter being earthed. G G are connected to ringing keys H H, and from thence to operator's set, which is included directly in the circuit.

To allow the operator to speak when answering a call with a single cord, it is arranged that the plugs when resting on the table shall make an earth connection. This is attained by the metal of the plugs, which is prolonged past the vulcanite sleeve (as shown in Fig. 106), resting on metal plates or sockets screwed under

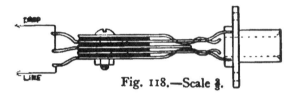

Fig. 118.—Scale ⅜.

the table, and connected to earth. This earth connection is severed directly the cord is raised.

The ring-off drops are connected in shunt in order to get rid of the harmful effects of their electro-magnetic inertia, or self-induction, on the speaking. The self-induction even plays a useful part when the apparatus is connected as a shunt, as it offers a great resistance to the passage of rapid alternations of the speaking currents, whilst to the comparatively slow alternations of the ringing currents it offers little or no extra resist-

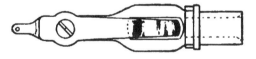

Fig. 119.—Scale ⅜.

ance. For this reason the self-induction of the ring-off drops is increased as much as possible, by using large and long cores for a single coil, and enclosing the latter

in a soft-iron tube, to form a box or armoured electro-
magnet.

A new pattern of spring-jack (Figs. 118 and 119) is
used on the later boards of the Western Electric
Company. The contacts are all doubled, two-line
springs being used, between which a connecting plug is
forced in making a connection, lifting the springs from
the central contact plate.

Single Cord Switch-boards.—These are made similar
in form to the "Standard," but each line is connected

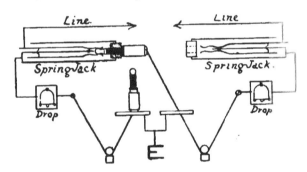

Fig. 120.

to a cord and plug, so that a 100-line board would be
provided with 100 cords and plugs. The connection of
two subscribers is accomplished by using the plug of
either of the subscribers to be connected, leaving in
circuit for ring-off purposes the drop belonging to the
line whose plug is thus used. This, of course, reduces
the time taken in making connections, and would appear
to be a great advantage, but this merit is neutralised in
some forms of the board by the number of operations
necessary in answering and ringing by the operator.

Fig 120, represents the connections of two lines on a very good form of board made by the Western Electric Company. The shanks of all the subscribers' plugs are insulated by a sleeve of ebonite, as shown in Fig. 121, so that when inserted in a spring-jack they only make contact with the line spring. The operator uses for answering the calls a double plug and cord, Fig. 122, to which her instrument and ringing generator are connected by means of a Dewar key, as shown in Fig. 123. On a drop falling, the operator inserts her plug in the subscriber's jack, and her instru-

Fig. 121.
Scale ⅔.

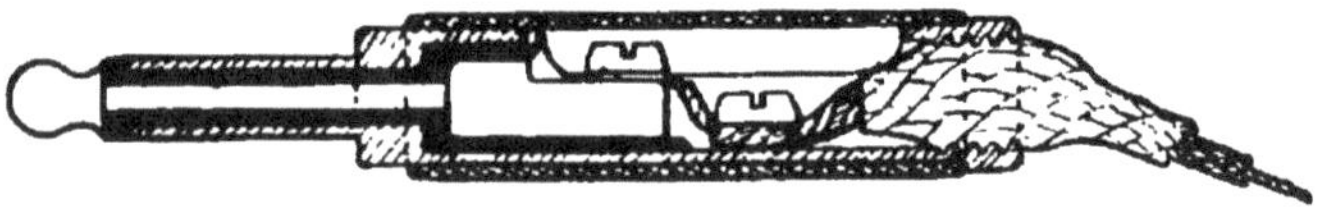

Fig. 122.—Scale ⅔.

ment is then connected directly in the circuit. The calling subscriber's plug is next inserted in the jack

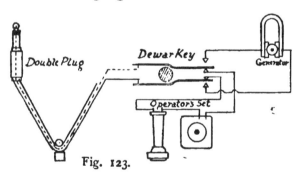

Fig. 123.

of the number required; the operator turns over the

Dewar key and rings through both lines, and when she hears them commence conversation, she disconnects herself by taking out her plug.

Operators' Transmitters.—These should be small, as large ones, such as the ordinary Blake, hide a large part of the switch-board from the operator. Metal-cased Blakes, Figs. 39 and 40, are often used. A good form of suspension is shown in Fig. 113, the connections to it being made by the flexible suspending copper ropes, which pass over ebonite pulleys carried on a horizontal arm capable of adjustment. The weight of the transmitter is balanced by one or two lead weights, so that the transmitter may be adjusted in a moment to whatever height may be desirable.

The ebonite pulleys should not be too small, as the continual bending to which the suspending wires are subjected in passing over them is very severe, and rapidly wears them through, unless pulleys of not less than 1 inch dia. are used. The flexible wire is made up of a large number of copper wires, about 6 or 7 mils dia., stranded together. It should offer little resistance, for being in the primary circuit it would otherwise affect the efficiency of the transmitter.

Another plan sometimes adopted is shown in Fig. 124. Speaking is done through a brass tube, fitted by a ball-and-socket joint in the mouth of the Blake. The tube can be adjusted in all directions. This plan has the drawback that it never looks straight and tidy, and the Blake, being firmly fixed to the top of the board, is liable to respond to all its vibrations.

In small exchanges Leclanché cells are used for the working of the operator's transmitters, and to keep them in good order it is necessary that they should be given

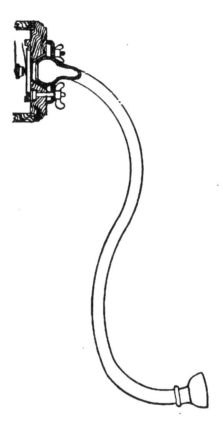

Fig. 124.—Scale ⅛.

frequent intervals of rest, as they are heavily worked. Arrangements are therefore used which, when the receiver is not in use, automatically cause a break in the primary circuit.

Fig. 125 shows a device introduced by the writer for the above purpose. When the receiver is not in use it is laid on prong B, carried in an ebonite bush, A, let into

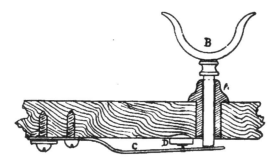

Fig. 125.—Scale ⅛.

the switch-table. Its weight presses down the spring C from a platinum contact on the brass plate D ; C and D form part of the primary circuit of the transmitter.

An ingenious plan for the same purpose, called *Gray's Contact Breaker*, is shown in Fig. 126. The receiver is

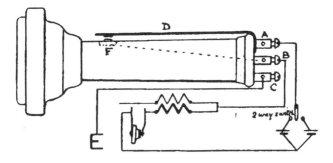

Fig. 126.—Scale ⅛.

furnished with three terminals, A B C. Under A is fastened the flat spring D. From B a wire extends to a contact plate, F. The connections to the transmitter are shown

in the figures, and it will be seen that the connection to
B is common to both the secondary and primary circuits.
The operator, in taking up the instrument, closes the
primary circuit by pressing D against F. An objection
to this form is that the flexible tinsel telephone cord is
introduced into the primary
circuit, the resistance of
which is rather high, and
gets higher with use. The
operator has always to grasp
the instrument in the same
manner, and she is always in
circuit with the secondary
circuit, which is objectionable during lightning storms.

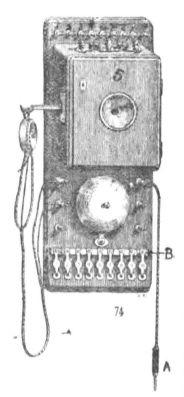

Fig. 127.

In addition to the above
arrangements, it is desirable
to provide a two-way switch in
the primary circuit, joined
up to two cells, so that the
operator may, by moving over
the switch now and then
during the day, change the
working cell. The connec-
tions for this are shown in
Fig. 126.

Domestic Switch-boards.—Fig. 127 shows an instrument made by the Western Electric Company, designed
for the joining up by telephones of a number of rooms in
the same or adjoining buildings, so that a person at any

one station may ring and speak to any other one without the aid of an ordinary switch-board and operator.

To accomplish this an instrument like Fig. 127, which comprises switch-bell, microphone, and switch-board, is fixed in each office, each instrument being numbered. A wire from every one station to every other one is run through and attached to the terminal at the top of the instrument corresponding to its number. If ten offices

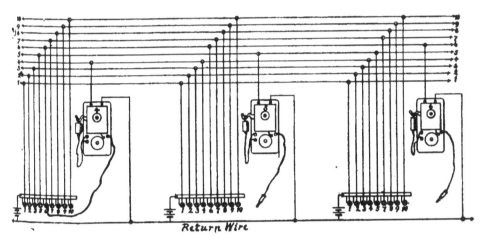

Fig. 128.

are to be connected, ten wires will be run, making the circuit of the whole, and an eleventh wire will be needed for the return circuit if earth is not used. The terminals are connected to sockets let into the bottom of the instrument, into which the plug A, connected to the telephone set, fits without touching the springs 1, 2, 3, etc., screwed on a bar, B, which is connected to one end of a battery.

L

The figure represents the No. 5 instrument, and it will be observed that the No. 5 socket and spring are absent, No. 5 line being connected direct to the instru-

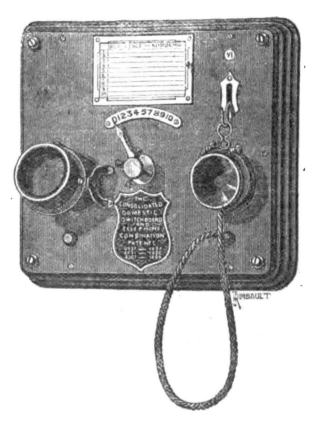

Fig. 129.

ment terminal. When No. 6 requires No. 4, the No. 4 spring on No. 6 instrument is pressed against the socket, causing No. 4 bell to ring. No. 6 then puts his instrument plug into No. 4 socket, and will be in communication with the person at No. 4, when the latter takes up his receiver.

Fig. 128 gives the connections for three stations. Wires with coverings of different colours should be used in running the lines so as to render the tracing of them easy.

A very neat instrument for the same purpose, made by the Consolidated Telephone Company, is shown in Fig. 129. Instead of a plug and cord, a handle-switch is used to connect to the different lines, and an automatic arrangement is adopted by which, on the hanging up of the receiver, the switch handle is released and a spring pulls it back to No. 0, its normal position.

CHAPTER VIII.

MULTIPLE SWITCH-BOARDS.

In a large telephonic exchange, where more than three or four switch-boards similar to those described in the last chapter are employed, the connection of any two subscribers out of the reach of the operator who answers the call gives rise to much trouble and delay. Some means of communicating between the operators on different tables has to be adopted, and whichever way this communication is accomplished time and trouble are expended, and the connection is delayed.

To overcome this difficulty the *multiple board* was invented, the principle of which is that, instead of having to connect any one subscriber at some one invariable position in the exchange, as in the old form of board, by the multiple any subscriber can be joined to any other *at every table in the central office*. The connecting places of subscribers are therefore multiplied, hence the name *multiple*. Any operator can connect *any* two subscribers together without moving more than a step, thus getting rid of the complicated methods of

Fig. 130.

connecting and at least one-half the number of operations necessary on the other switch-boards, when the lines to be joined were not on the same table.

Many multiple systems have been invented, but the only one which has been extensively employed so far is that of the Western Electric Company, in the perfecting of which a large amount of ingenuity and inventiveness has been exhibited.

Since its first introduction the board has undergone many modifications, but it now appears to have settled down into something of a standard shape, of which Fig. 130, representing a *table*, or *section*, of the Manchester board, will give an idea. The upper portion of the table is divided into six panels. In these six panels is fitted a spring-jack for each subscriber whose wire is centred in the switch-room. The spring-jacks are arranged in groups of 100, made up of five horizontal rows of 20. Each group is numbered from 1 to 100, a number painted on the framework of the panels denoting the particular hundred. The first group (the bottom left-hand one) is numbered 0, the next to the right 1, the next 2, and so on to the sixth panel; then another row above from left to right, thus building upwards. These groups are called the *ordinary* jacks, to distinguish from the 200 *local* jacks arranged along the length of the table just below. The local spring-jacks are those into which the operators plug in answering the calls of the subscribers whose wires terminate on the table. They correspond to the jacks in the "Standard" switch-board described in last chapter.

The indicator drops in connection with the local jacks are arranged at a lower level, in four groups of 50, making 200 in all, which is the number of subscribers whose lines are terminated on each table, and whose calls are answered by the three operators attending to it.

Between the local jacks and the drops a ledge or

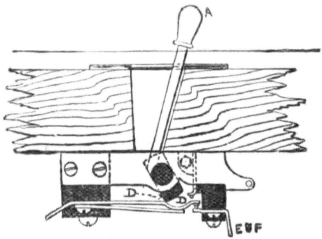

Fig. 131.—Scale ¼.

shelf is formed, through holes in which the connecting cords pass, the plugs attached to them resting when not in use on brass earth-plates screwed underneath the shelf. The brass prolongation of the plug thus makes earth, as in the " Standard." The cords are arranged in pairs, one in front of the other. Connected to, and in a vertical line beneath each pair, is a ring-off drop, fixed below the calling drops. On another shelf, just below, a *Werner* table-switch and two ringing keys are provided for each of the 45 pairs of cords. The cords and accessories are arranged in three groups of 15 for the operators who attend to each table. The Werner table-switch, Figs. 131 and 132, answers the same purpose as the Dewar switch already described.

As many sections or tables as there are multiples of

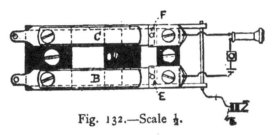

Fig. 132.—Scale ½.

200 subscribers connected in the switch-room are fixed end to end to form a complete multiple board.

Engaged Test.—As in a multiple board there may be many sections, on each of which any subscriber in the room may be connected, it is evident that some means is required, before connecting a subscriber's line on any one table, of ascertaining if the wire is already connected on another section, or one wire may get connected to several others at the same time, and lead to trouble and confusion. A *test* for this is a necessity in any multiple system.

The means by which the test is made in the Western Electric Company's board can be explained by reference to Fig. 133, which gives a sketch of the connections of a subscriber's line, and Fig. 134, which gives the connec-tions of the operator's instruments. It will be seen from the latter that, in addition to the operator's ordinary instruments, a *test cell* is included in the *line or secondary circuit* of the telephone.

The subscriber's line is connected to the spring of his jack on the first section of the board. From the back contact of this the line goes to the spring of the corresponding jack on the next section, and so on until the whole of the jacks belonging to the same number, including the local jack, have been so connected. The

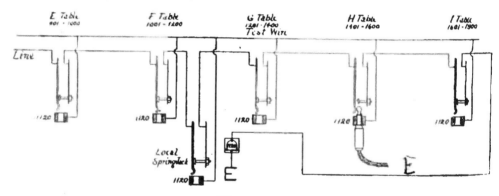

Fig. 133.

back contact of the last spring-jack is connected to the earthed indicator on the same table as the local jack. Fig. 133 shows the connections of No. 1,120 line at the last five tables. Besides the line connections, it will be seen that the sockets of the spring-jacks are insulated, and are all connected to a separate wire, which is called the *test* or *click* wire, which is carefully insulated.

On the insertion of a plug at any one of the jacks the socket is thereby connected to the line, and gets earth through the subscriber's instrument. The effect of the insertion of a plug is shown at the H table, where we suppose the line is connected to some other number. All the jacks behind the H table and the drop are cut out from the line connection, which is diverted to the plug and cord. If 1,120 is now asked for on another table, the operator having turned over the table switch, so as to put her telephone set in connection with the pair of cords she is using, and having her receiver to her ear, takes up the second plug of the pair (the first being

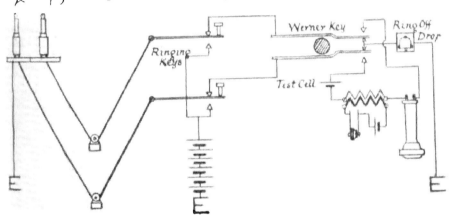

Fig. 134.

already connected to the calling subscriber's line), and before pressing it into No. 1,120's jack, taps the end of the plug on the socket of the jack. If she then hears a click in her receiver, she knows that the number is engaged on another section, as would be the case in this instance. The click is caused by the test cell getting a complete circuit through No. 1,120's test wire and the lines of the two subscribers. If the number had been disengaged, the test wire and sockets would remain insulated, no click would have been heard, and the operator would have completed the connection by pressing in the plug.

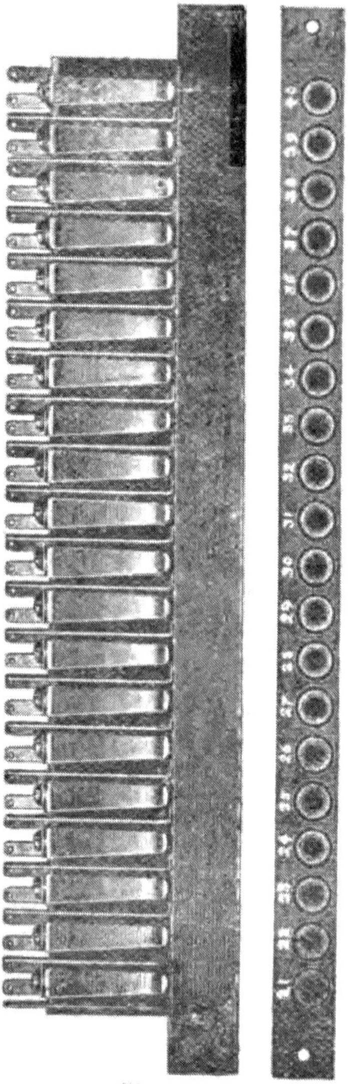

Thus a fraction of a second suffices to find out if a subscriber's line is engaged at any part of the room.

Spring-jacks.—Two sizes and arrangements of these are used in multiple boards, the larger, shown in Fig. 105, is made so that each one is complete in itself. The smaller size, which is used on most of the later multiple boards, is made up in sets of twenty, the springs, sockets, and contact screws of the set being fitted on strips of ebonite, and form a very neat and compact arrangement, as shown in Figs. 135 and 136, the latter being a section. The strips are secured to the framework of the tables by a screw at each end of the strip, so that their fixture or removal is a much simpler matter than that of the separate jacks. The

Fig. 135.

insulation of the jacks on the strips is very good, which is important in a large exchange where each line is connected to a number of jacks, each forming a point for leakage. Being more enclosed, the contacts are much better protected from dust, which is a great advantage, as most of the trouble met with in switch-boards arises from dust settling on the contacts. Another good point is that the space occupied on the tables is only about one-half that of the larger-sized jacks, 100 small jacks taking up 40 square inches, and 100 of the larger ones 80 square inches. The latter point governs the number of jacks which can be fitted into any one section, so that the operators and the connect-ing cords can reach to connect, and thus settles the number of

Fig. 136.—Scale ¼.

subscribers which can be provided for in one centre, or what is called the *ultimate capacity* of the board. The ultimate capacity of the Manchester board, Fig. 130, is 4,200, but it is only at present fitted for 1,800 lines.

Cabling or Wiring.—The great number of connections that have to be made to the jacks necessitates the adoption of some definite plan of dealing with the mass of wires in order to avoid confusion. The number of connections increases as the square of the number of lines in the centre, so that a compact method of wiring is especially necessary in a large exchange.

The method of wiring adopted should allow of the jacks being readily accessible in case of faults.

The shorter the length of wire used the better, as

both dynamic and static induction increase with the length.

The wires used should not impede access to other parts of the tables, and they should occupy as little space as possible.

The cables used are oval in section, $\frac{1}{2}$ in. × $\frac{3}{4}$ in., each containing 21 *pairs* of wires, which provide for both the line and test wires of a row of 20 jacks. Each pair of wires is twisted together, one being for the line wire and the other for the test, being distinguished by different coloured coverings.

The lengths of cable for each 20 lines are so connected to the jacks, and bound up together, from one end of the board to the other, that they look like a single straight cable with strips of jacks fastened at regular intervals (equal to the width of a section = about 6$\frac{1}{2}$ feet). The fitting to the jacks is done apart from the switch-board on a long bench fitted with *forming blocks*, one of which is shown in Fig. 137 (which also shows the underside of a strip of jacks), fixed at distances apart equal to the width of the sections of the board. In this manner the joints can be more carefully soldered and inspected than if they had to be done in position behind the tables, as was the case with the former system of cabling.

The *forming block*, Fig. 137, is made up of a block of wood D (fixed to the bench), to which the strip of jacks is temporarily screwed. F F is a smaller wooden block, from the top of which 20 small iron pins project, round which the wires are bent in connecting

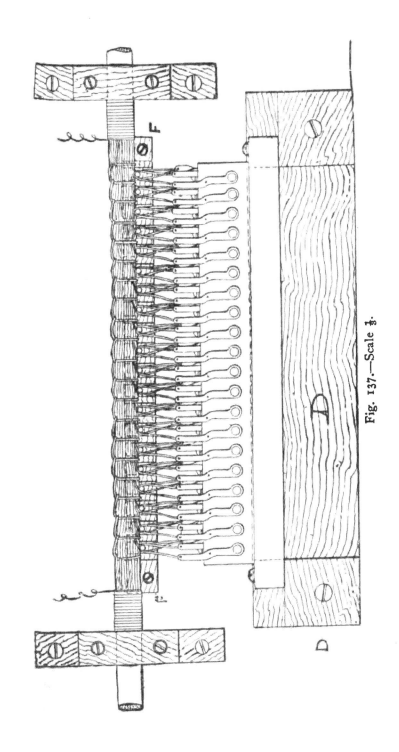

F

D

D

Fig. 137.—Scale ⅓.

to the jacks. The lengths of cables (which are rather longer than the width of the switch-board sections), whilst being connected to the jacks, are fixed in the clamps shown, a length of cable coming from each side. Testing for the proper wires is done by means of plugs and cords connected to a battery and bell, so that the bell sounds when the same wire is touched by a plug at each end.

When a whole length has thus been connected,

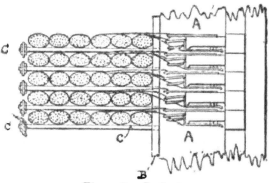

Fig. 138.—Scale ¼.

soldered and tested, and the wires bound up as shown, it is released from the forming blocks, lifted off the pegs in F F, carried to its position behind the tables, and the jacks screwed in their proper places. Fig. 138 gives a section of the cables required to fit up 600 lines, being 30 cables for 30 rows of jacks, and shows how they are supported by steel rods c c, screwed into steel strips, B. A A is an end view of five rows of jacks in one panel.

Fig. 139 shows how the cables are arranged one behind the other by making the connecting wires from the

cables to the rows of jacks in six
lengths, differing from each other by
¾ in., the width of the cable. By this
method the cables are very compactly
arranged, the shortest possible length
of cable is needed, access to the
other parts of the tables is not
impeded in the least, and the strips
of jacks can be brought out behind
for inspection and the remedying of
faults.

*Scribner's Single-Cord Multiple
Board.*—This is a board also made
by the W. E. Co., in which a plug and
cord is provided for each subscriber's
line, as before described. As shown
by Fig. 140, which gives the connections of two lines and the operator's set, it is rather complicated.
It is no doubt this fact which has
prevented its coming into more
general use.

The plugs in their normal position
are held fast within the so-called
earth-switch c, by a weight and pulley.
The *lever switches a* serve for connecting and disconnecting the operator's
set, and also for ringing up the called-
for subscriber. A special call-key,
b^1, and b^2, with plug and cord

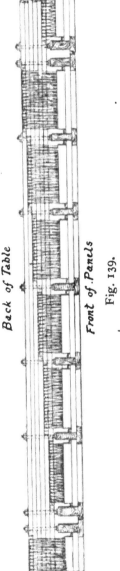

Back of Table *Front of Panels* Fig. 139.

connections, *b*, enables an operator to assist an over-burdened colleague.

The working is as follows :—As soon as the operator sees, say, drop *h*, fall, she lifts up plug *i*, thereby connecting her telephone to the line. After receiving instructions, she taps *i* on the socket of the subscriber wanted, and, if engaged, gets the ordinary test click. If

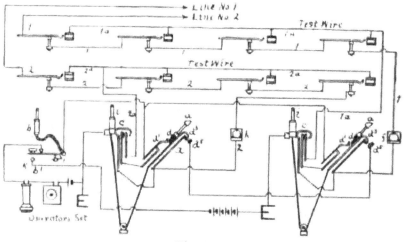

Fig. 140.

free, she inserts the plug, and to ring him up depresses the button *a*, so as to bring the spring d^3 on to battery or generator contact d^5. After thus connecting, the operator cuts out her own instrument by pressing the ebonite block *d* under spring d^1 by means of the button *a*.

The ordinary indicator drop of the calling subscriber serves as the ring-off drop. As it is spoken through, its coils should be joined up in multiple to lessen the self-induction.

It is advisable to provide double cords and switches in conjunction with the operator's set in case of accident, and to better assist neighbouring operators.

One hundred subscribers are allotted to each operator.

Although the above board has a great advantage in the fewness of the motions necessary to make a connection, and the consequent rapidity, there are many drawbacks in connection with it, which have prevented its being used to any great extent.

A strong objection to single-cord boards is that they cannot be converted into metallic circuit boards, which will be important in the future.

The largest central office in the world is that of Hamburg, which is fitted for 6,200 lines, is worked on the single-cord multiple system, and appears to have given much satisfaction.

M

CHAPTER IX.

SPECIAL EXCHANGE SYSTEMS.

IN this chapter a few telephonic systems which have special features differing from the ordinary run of telephonic exchanges will be briefly described.

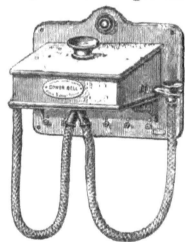

Fig. 141.

British Post Office System.— The system adopted at Newcastle, and other places where the Post Office authorities have established telephonic exchanges, is of a novel and interesting character.

The instruments used by the subscribers are the Gower receiver and transmitter. These, together with the automatic switches, etc., are arranged in a case, as seen in Fig. 141, the signalling being done by batteries.

Fig. 142 gives a view of the interior of the case with the cover removed, and **Fig. 143** the connections of batteries and other parts.

R is the magnet of the receiver, I the transmitter induction coil of resistances :—primary ·5, and secondary 250 ohms. SS' are two automatic prong switches, in which the ear-pieces of the flexible tubes are placed when not in use. The right-hand one serves to break the local microphone circuit, the left-hand lever is the usual bell and telephone automatic. K is the ringing button, B a Post Office relay for operating the local

Fig. 142.

bell. Six terminals are fixed at the bottom of the case. Between ZE and C are connected the two Leclanché cells required for the microphone. Between BC and ZE five Daniell cells. When the left-hand lever is down this battery is permanently connected to line. This constitutes the peculiarity of the system, as it is worked on the *closed circuit* system, a battery current always passing through the line when the instrument is not in use. No earth is used to the

instrument, double or metallic circuits being almost
exclusively employed, and are absolutely necessary,
owing to the fact that the lines are run in close proximity. to single-wire telegraph circuits, the induction
from which on single-wire telephone lines would render

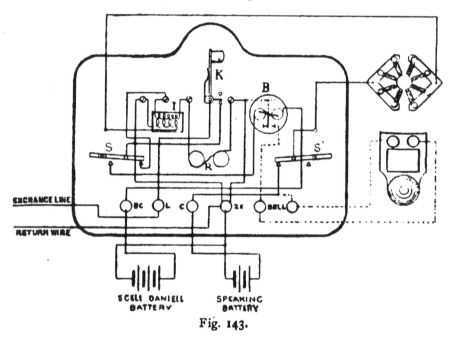

Fig. 143.

the voice nearly or quite inaudible.   The use of metallic
circuits for the purpose of suppressing induction will be
referred to in Chapter XII.

Central Office Apparatus.—The subscriber's lines on
entering the switch-room are connected to a special
form of indicator, shown in Figs. 144 and 145.   The
electro-magnet M M is screwed to a ring of brass, which
forms the framework of the drop.   In a boss at the

bottom of this a pillar is fitted, to which is pivoted at *a* the thin iron washer A A, which forms the drop shutter. Whilst a current passes through the coils, A A is held in the position shown by the attraction, but on the current ceasing A A drops until its lower edge rests against the insulated pin S'S, to which a local night-bell circuit is attached.

Fig. 144.

Between the poles of the magnet a small magnetic needle, *i*, is suspended, which is attracted to one pole or other of M M, according to their polarity. A card of the shape shown is fixed behind A, on which the number, etc., is written. Under normal conditions, when the line is not in use, the needle points to the left, as shown. If the line

Fig. 145.—Scale ½.

current ceases by the subscriber taking up the tubes, A A falls, and the needle points to the centre of the card, which indicates to the operator that the subscriber desires attention. The operator answers by inserting a flat double plug attached to her instru-

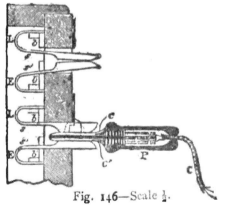

Fig. 146—Scale ¼.

ment into a kind of flat spring-jack, both being shown in Fig. 146. C C' are two strips of brass fastened on

the two sides of a piece of ebonite, the double connecting
cord c is attached to c c', and to the two terminals of the
operator's instrument. s and s' are two brass pieces
attached to springs which form the jack, normally being
in contact with each other, as shown at the top of the
figure. A double cord, with a plug like P at each end, is
used to connect two subscribers.

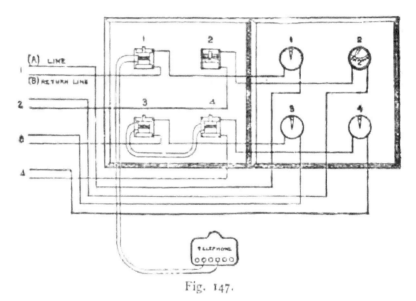

Fig. 147.

Fig. 147 shows the connection for four lines, the
indicators at the right and the connecting jacks at the
left.   Lines 3 and 4 are shown connected together
with both indicators left in circuit. Line 1 is shown
connected to the operator's set, and line 2 normal.

To call up the subscribers a strong battery is used at
the central office, which, together with the subscriber's
battery, is sufficiently powerful to actuate the relay in

the subscriber's instrument, which has been so biased by means of a spring that the subscriber's battery is not in itself strong enough to actuate it.

The ring-off signal is automatically given by the subscribers hanging up the tubes and thus reconnecting the permanent current to line, which deflects the needle magnet at the central office.

Subscribers may be furnished with a commutator with which to reverse the permanent current going to line, and cause the indicator needle to point to the right, which indicates to the operator that the subscriber is leaving his office.

The permanent current is also a permanent test as to the state of the line or instrument, a fault happening to them deranging the current.

Although a very perfect system for a small exchange, its advantages are dearly bought, as the frequent attention necessary to the Daniell batteries and the constant waste of material constitute very serious drawbacks.

Manchester National Telephone Company's System.— The exchange in connection with the National Telephone Company at Manchester is worked by batteries combined with apparatus by means of which a special ring-off system is arranged, enabling each subscriber to call up any other when connected without the intervention of the operators, and without actuating the ring-off signal. This arrangement overcomes the difficulty which is met with in exchanges having no special ring-off system (which is the case with most exchanges), that the subscribers, if they do not at once get through to the subscribers they ask for, will persist in ringing themselves, notwithstanding that the effect of this is to cause the ring-off drop to fall at the exchange, much annoyance ensuing to both subscribers and operators.

The Manchester system was invented and brought into use in 1880 by the writer. The subscribers are each furnished with a set of instruments, comprising

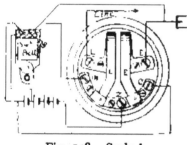

Blake transmitter, Bell receiver, switch-bell (Silvertown or Liverpool pattern), and a special *commutator press-button*, by means of which the current sent from the battery is reversed in direction to that sent by the ordinary signalling button.

Fig. 148.—Scale ⅛.

Fig. 149.—Scale ⅓.

The commutator button is shown in Figs. 148 and 149, the former being a plan with the cover and button removed, and showing the connections to the switch-bell and battery. L and E are two doubled back brass springs connected respectively to line and earth, with their ends normally making contact on the brass plates I N and Z. Plate Z also passes under the end of L spring, and under the end of E is the plate C. On pressing the ordinary ringing button the carbon end of the battery is connected to line, and the zinc end to earth through the spring E. On pressing the commu-

Fig. 151.

tator button the L spring is brought into contact with Z and the zinc end of the battery, and the E spring with C and the carbon end, thus sending a reversed current to line. The commutator button is black and the ordinary one white, to distinguish them.

Polarized Ring-off Drop.—The ring-off drop at the central office is polarized by a permanent magnet (somewhat similarly to the magneto polarized bell), and is so arranged that it only responds to a current from the zinc end of the battery, and is neutral to a copper current.

The ring-off drops are connected each to a pair of cords and table switch in such a manner that they form a shunt to earth, as shown in Fig. 132. They have a good amount of iron about them, and are wound to a resistance of about 100 ohms, so that they have considerable electro-magnetic inertia, and therefore offer considerable impedance to the speaking currents.

The above system has given great satisfaction to the subscribers, especially since it was allied with the W. E. Co.'s multiple switch-board, which was fitted up at the Royal Exchange in 1888, under the superintendence of the writer, forming a switch-room so complete that it is still looked upon as the model centre of the United Kingdom.

A general view of the room is given in Fig. 150, the boards on the right being the ordinary multiple tables, and those at right angles in the back-ground the trunk-line switch-boards.

Further details of the arrangement are given in Chapters VIII. and X.

Paris Exchange System.—Metallic circuits are used in Paris, the wires, in the form of cables, being run in the very extensive system of sewers for which the city is famed.

The battery system is exclusively employed, the subscribers being furnished with a set of instruments, comprising an Ader transmitter and receiver, a relay, an automatic switch, two special forms of signalling buttons or keys, and a battery of 9 Leclanché cells.

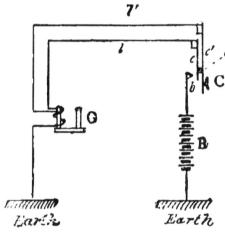

Fig. 151.

The two buttons serve the same purpose as those described in connection with the Manchester system, but the method of actuating the ring off-drop is different. Figs. 151, 152 and 153 will help to explain the method of working. Fig. 151 shows the arrangement for answering a call or calling a subscriber by the operator at the central office. The operator makes connection to the subscriber's line by a double cord and plug, as in the Newcastle system, then depresses a key C, composed of two springs, *c* and *c'*, which, on pressure, come into contact through the metal piece *d* attached to *c'*. By this means the two ends of the lines *l* and *l'* are connected to the earthed battery B, and a current is sent through the subscriber's relay G to earth, the two line wires being used as a single one of double conductivity.

When two subscribers' lines are connected together by two double plugs and cords, their drops are joined

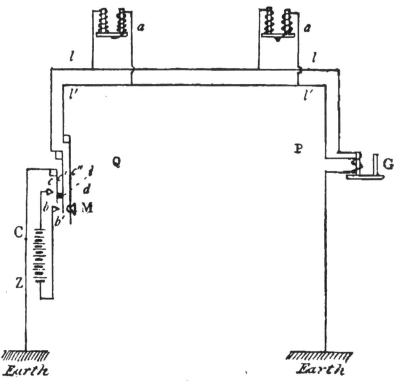

Fig. 152.

up in loop or derived circuit between the metallic circuit wires, as shown at *a a* in Fig. 152, which shows two subscribers, Q and P, joined together through the exchange. If Q wishes to ring P, he uses the button M', by which three springs, *c c'* and *c"*, are depressed on to the two battery contacts, *b* and *b'*, *c'* and *c"* coming into contact by the operation, whilst *c* and *c'* are insulated from each other. The effect of this is to put one end of the battery to earth, and send a current from the other end through the *two wires as a single line*, and through the relay of P at the other end without affecting the drops *a a* at the central office, which are only operated by the key M, shown in Fig. 153, which sends a current through the metallic circuit of the line.

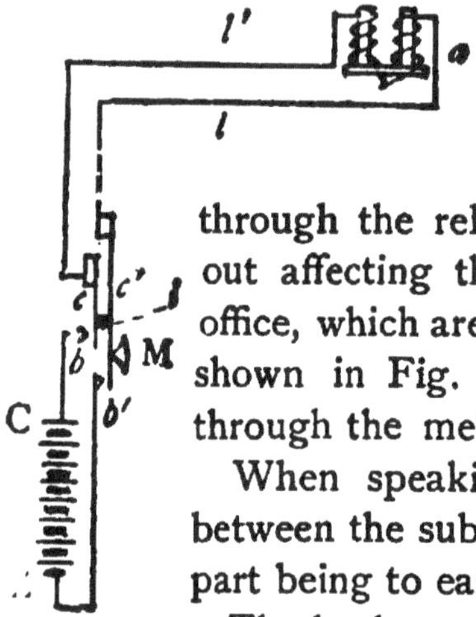

When speaking, the circuit all through between the subscribers is a metallic one, no part being to earth.

Fig. 153.

The back contacts of the ringing keys are not shown, but will be understood when it is mentioned that the springs *c'* and *c"* of Fig. 152, and

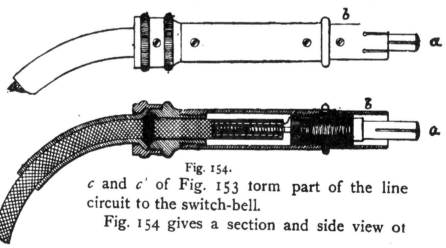

Fig. 154.

c and *c'* of Fig. 153 form part of the line circuit to the switch-bell.

Fig. 154 gives a section and side view of

the double plug used at the central office to make the connections.

The split plug *a* is connected to one wire of the cord, and the metal cylinder *b* to the other conductor, *a* and *b* being insulated from each other.

Figs. 155 and 156 show the *jack* used, which consists of two thick brass plates, insulated from each other by a thin strip of ebonite, and fastened together by the two

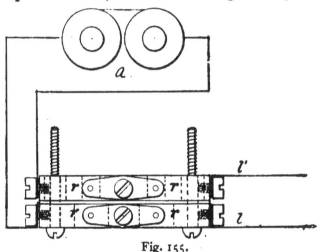

Fig. 155.

screws shown. Two holes are drilled in each plate, those in the front one large enough for the outside of the plug, and those in the back one for the small part of the plug. The connections to the drop *a* and to the lines *l l'* are shown in Fig. 155. The springs *r r* are furnished with phosphor-bronze pins, which project slightly into the plug holes, and ensure good contact on to the plugs when these are inserted. No contacts are broken when the plug is inserted, a derived circuit only is connected to the former circuit through the drops.

Since the French Government took over the telephones in 1890 many changes have been made in Paris. A large exchange is in course of erection, into which the lines of most of the twelve central offices at present established will be concentrated. For the new exchange a multiple switch-board for 6,000 lines will be provided.

This concentration of lines into large central offices is the feature of the telephonic exchange work of the present, and gets rid of much of the complication and delay attendant upon the use of the trunk lines joining various scattered centres.

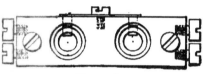
Fig. 156.

The Law System.—This system differs materially from the ordinary methods of working telephonic exchanges. Together with similar systems, and in combination with the multiple system, it seems destined to play a great part in the telephone world of the future. The inventor was Mr. F. Shaw, of the Law Telegraph Company, New York.

Beside the ordinary subscribers' line, a second line is run, which joins up successively every subscriber's office within a certain area, as shown in Fig. 157, and again returns to the central office. As many of these special group lines or *call wires* are run as will be sufficient to join all the subscribers, each call line joining from 50 to 100. During the day an operator is continually listening on each of the call wires, and the subscribers are all furnished with switches, by means of which they can connect themselves on to one of the call wires, and thus be able to tell the listening operator which number they wish to speak with, giving their own number at the same time. The subscriber's ordinary wire is then joined by the operator to that of the subscriber he wishes, by means of two plugs and a cord. The caller turns back his switch to his ordinary

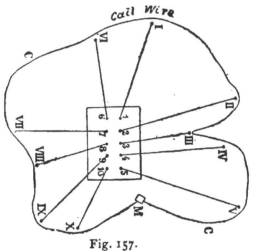

Fig. 157.

line, rings through to the called subscriber, and, when his conversation is finished, again connects himself to the call wire, and tells the operator to disconnect.

So long as proper connection on the wires is ensured this system is very simple and effective, the subscribers being always in touch with the operators at the central office, and, as in the connection with subscribers no drop indicator is necessary, the speaking on the lines is very good. Unfortunately, the method of connecting up the call wire gave rise to faults, which would disarrange a whole group of subscribers ; a simple break on any part of the call line, or in any of the switches employed, affecting the whole of the subscribers joined up on it.

Mann System.—A different method of connecting up

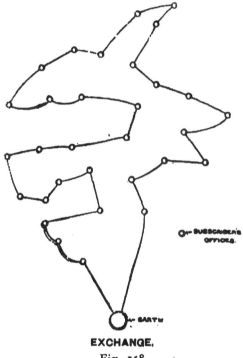

O← SUBSCRIBER'S OFFICES.

←EARTH

EXCHANGE.

Fig. 158.

the subscribers to the call wire, introduced by Mr. J. J. Mann, avoided these breakdowns, and has given great satisfaction at Dundee, where the system has been employed for some years. In the Law system the subscribers were joined to the call wire *in series*, no earth being employed, whilst by the Mann system the subscribers are joined in derived circuits to earth when they turn over their switches. A main branch of the call wire is run through a central part of the group, and branches from this are carried to each of the sub- scribers' offices.

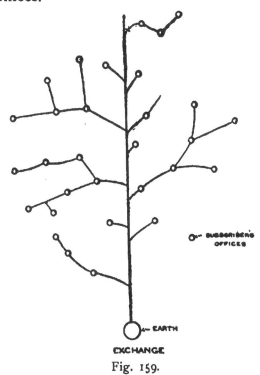

Fig. 159.

The difference is shown by Figs. 158 and 159, the former of which represents the Law and the latter the Mann call wire for joining up the same 31 stations.

The switch for connecting to the call wire is shown in Fig. 160. The switch-room end of the call wire is to earth through the operator's set during the busy

N

hours of the day, but during the night and other slack
times the operator ceases to listen, and a battery and
bell are switched in connection with the call wire, as
shown in Fig. 161 (the wire marked "operator's line"
being the end of the call wire). On a subscriber pressing down his switch, the call wire gets earth, and the

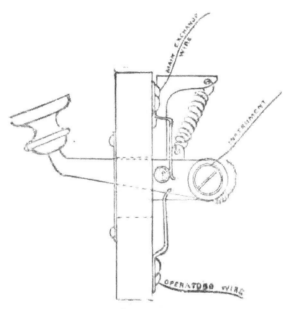

Fig. 160.

bell rings and attracts the operator's attention. Indicator drops need not be used at all in connection
with the subscribers' lines, but at Dundee they are
provided so that, in case of accident to the call wires,
the subscribers may signal in the ordinary manner.
It is evidence of very good service that these drops are
seldom or never used.

On the Mann system only an earth fault or disconnection on the main call wire 'near the central office could disconnect all the subscribers joined to it. A fault occurring usually only affects a few subscribers of the group. Nevertheless, particular care should be

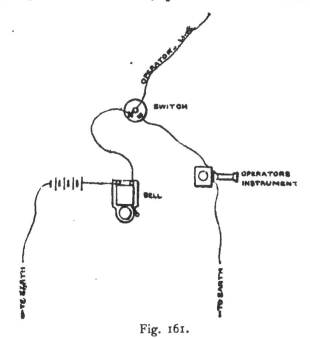

Fig. 161.

taken to keep the call wire free from faults by running it well above and apart from other wires.

The Mutual Telephone Company's Manchester System. —A very complete and effective system has lately been installed in Manchester by the above company. It combines the Mann system with metallic circuits and the multiple principle, and seems as near a perfect telephone exchange as one can conceive.

The lines are run in specially manufactured overhead cables. Three wires go into each subscriber's office, two to form the subscriber's own metallic circuit, and the other to form a connection to the call wire. The calbes used generally contain 36 pairs of wires, each pair being twisted together, and one call wire run in the centre, making 73 wires in all.

Each subscriber is provided with a set of instruments, comprising a magneto bell for ringing other subscribers, a double polar receiver, and, since July, 1891, with a specially-designed carbon transmitter.

Normally, the metallic circuit wires are connected to the magneto bell as one wire, an earth circuit being used for ringing, as in the Paris system. When the receiver is taken up, the earth is cut off, and the speaking instruments are included directly in the metallic loop. A similar switch to Fig. 160, but rather more complicated, is used by the subscriber to connect himself to the call wire and listening operator.

The arrangements at the central office are very simple. No drops being necessary, the subscribers' lines are simply connected to a series of double sockets. The latter are made up in groups of 100, constructed as follows :—A slab of ebonite 5 in. square and $\frac{1}{4}$ in. thick is studded with 100 round brass sockets in ten rows of ten in each. Above this slab, and separated from it by a small space, is fixed a similar slab, in which 100 larger sockets, having larger holes, are fixed. One wire of a subscriber's double line is connected to a socket in the top slab, and the other to the socket immediately below.

Connection is made by double plugs and double cords, something like those in Fig. 154, but made on a smaller scale.

The sets of 100 connecting sockets are fixed horizontally in recesses made in a long table, so that they can be reached by operators on both sides of the latter, which is 28 in. wide.   Each of the sets has a large number painted on it, to distinguish the particular hundred, and each hundred is multipled, or repeated, along the table about every 5 ft., the sockets of any one number being connected by branches from the subscribers' lines, not in series, as in Fig. 133.

A special and ingenious engaged test is provided, so that the operators may learn at once if a subscriber is connected at some other part of the board.

The switch-board described above is the invention of Mr. A. R. Bennett, the general manager of the Mutual Telephone Company, to whom is also due the system of working adopted. A somewhat similar switch-board, but for single wires, has been in use at the Aberdeen centre of the National Telephone Company for about two years with the greatest success.

CHAPTER X.

TEST-ROOM APPLIANCES.

ALL the larger telephonic exchanges should be provided with a *test-room*, adjoining the switch-room, through which all lines should pass, special provision being made for testing the lines and the detection and locating of faults with the utmost dispatch.

The appliances which go to make up a complete test-room are as follows :—

1. *Test-Board*, to which all the lines are connected, special arrangements being made for quickly connecting the testing instruments to any lines.

2. *Lightning Arrester Board*, which often forms part of the test-board.

3. *Cross-connecting* or *Distributing Board*, by means of which the switch-room wires may be re-arranged as regards connection with the line wire leaders, still keeping all the wires tidy and regular. This distributing board really includes the test-board, but it is convenient to distinguish the two.

4. *Test-Clerk's Equipment*, which may be divided into two sets :—(*a*), Those required for rough testing purposes, such as contacts, breaks, etc. ; and (*b*) those for the more delicate tests of conductivity, insulation, and capacity of lines.

5. *Power Generator*, or pole-changer, for the production of ringing currents for the use of the operators. It is better to provide both these, so that one shall be available if the other fails. They should be fixed in the test-room, so as to be under the observation of the test-clerk in case of failure.

The appliances will be described in the order given above, and, to render the matter as clear as possible, the author's arrangement adopted at the Manchester Exchange of the National Telephone Company, which is the most complete in this country, will be selected for description, and other systems or appliances differing from it afterwards mentioned.

Test-board.—Three views of part of this are given in Figs. 162, 163, 164, drawn to a scale of one-half full size. Three strips of ebonite, A and B B, are connected together by screws buried in A. On the edges of B B are brass clips, D D, furnished with screws end washers. On one face of these the phosphor-bronze springs C C press. The latter are bent and clamped under the heads of screws, which pass through A, and on the other side are provided with nuts and washers, which help to clamp a brass plate forming part of the lightning arrester. Each complete block contains 40 of these springs, etc., 20 in each row. Ten blocks are screwed to a framework to

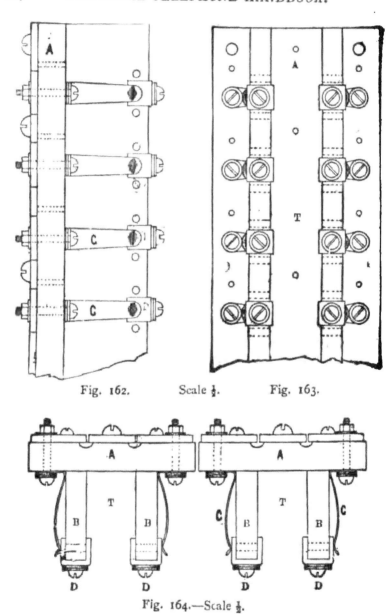

Fig. 162.　　Scale ½.　　Fig. 163.

Fig. 164.—Scale ½.

form one panel of the test-board, accommodating 400 lines.

Lightning Arrester Board.—The other side of the above blocks is shown in Fig. 165. E E is a brass strip screwed on to the ebonite. The serrated edges of the brass plates F F are clamped very close to but not touching E E, which is normally connected to earth by means of a plug at the bottom end. To prevent leakage between the plates F F and E, the ebonite is grooved out underneath, as shown in Fig. 164. To prevent leakage from the F plates on one block to those on the next, a small space is left when fixed, as also shown in Fig. 164.

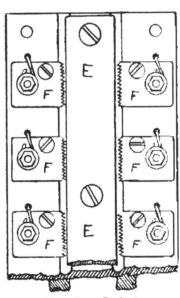

Fig. 165.—Scale ½.

It will be seen that when the blocks are fixed side by side, a series of troughs are formed. Into those, in which are the springs C C, the leads from the line wires are brought from a large trough fixed about 9 ft. from the floor. These are threaded through small holes to the other face of the block, and are there clamped to the plates F F.

Method of Using Test-board.—A shoe, constructed as shown in Fig. 166, is attached by a flexible cord to the testing set. A is a brass strip attached to the vulcanite strip B. On pressing this shoe between one of the

springs C, Fig. 164, and the brass plate on which its end
rests, the outside line or the inside line to the switch-board
(*via* the cross-connecting board) may be connected to the
test set, according to which way the shoe is turned.
Connections for testing are thus instantly made, no
wires having to be unscrewed and perhaps broken or
left loose, as with the old process of testing by double
terminals.   The   test   instrument   may   be   connected

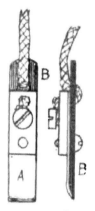

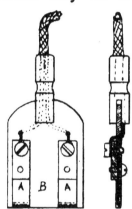

Fig. 166.—Scale ½.   Fig. 167.—Scale ⅜.

directly in the circuit of any line by using a shoe made
up of two brass strips with an insulating strip between,
the two terminals of the instrument being connected
to the brass strips.   For metallic circuit lines, the two
wires of which are led to adjacent terminals on the test-
board, a double test-shoe, as in Fig. 167, is used.

Cross-connecting Board.—Under the screws D, Fig.
164, wires are clamped which pass up through the
troughs T T and round the framework to the cross-
connecting board, part of which is shown in Figs. 168

and 169. It consists of a series of terminal plates, with screws and washers fitted in vertical lines on plates of ebonite (15 inches by 14 inches), grooved for the ends of the terminal plates, which are bent at right angles, so that they shall not turn. Two hundred plates are fitted to each in ten rows of 20, and three such complete blocks are fitted one over the other to form a complete

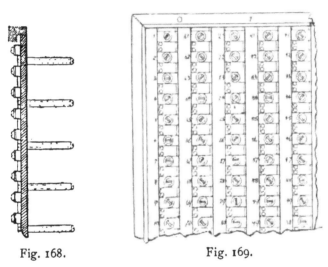

Fig. 168.   Fig. 169.

panel for 600 lines. The numbering is from top to bottom of the panel. The projecting pins at the back, covered with vulcanite sleeves, are used simply to form troughs to guide the wires and keep them tidy.

The wires from the switch-boards are brought in cables to the bottom of the board and up through the troughs, and are then connected to the terminal-plates in regular arithmetical order, so that any subscriber's number is the same as the number of the terminal to

which it is attached. On **the test-board this is not the**
case, the line wires being **attached to that board in the**
order in which they are **brought in, disregarding what**
subscriber they belong to.

The cross-connecting **board is arranged in a line**
with the switch-board, **and the test-board is placed at**
right angles. Connections
between the two are made
in a special manner, de-
signed to keep the wires
used for the purpose in an
orderly condition, and so
that they can readily be
taken out and others run
between different points of
the boards. This is managed
in the following manner :—
In a vertical line over *each*
of the troughs TT, Fig. 163,
a series of fourteen $\frac{7}{8}$-inch
holes are bored in the framework, as shown in Fig. 170.

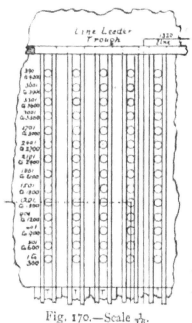

Fig. 170.—Scale $\frac{1}{18}$.

The connecting wires are
passed from the test-board through these holes, are then
led horizontally along and round the corner, until they
arrive over the part of the cross-connecting board on
which their numbers are situated, when they are
threaded through other holes and down to the terminal
plates. All connecting wires for subscribers whose
numbers are between 1 and 300 pass through the

lowest of the 14 holes in any trough. All between 300 and 600 pass through the second hole from the bottom, and so on, rising a hole higher for every 300 subscribers, so that the top or fourteenth row of holes will only be used when the full capacity of the switch-board (4,200 lines) is nearly attained. At present 1,600 subscribers are connected, and the sixth set of holes from the bottom is in use.

As the numbers on the test-board are no guide to the subscribers connected, it is necessary to provide a book in which two lists are given : (1) A list of subscribers in numerical order, showing the numbers on the test-board to which each one is connected ; and (2) the test-board number in numerical order, showing what subscribers are connected to each. A column is left in each list for recording alterations.

The Manchester installation, as given above, was the first occasion on which the distributing board was used in connection with the telephonic exchanges in this country, although it had for some years been considered indispensable to a complete system in the United States. Any one who has seen the awful tangle and confusion in which the leads are involved in any of the large exchanges not employing one would recognise its utility. The tangle was due to the fact that on the frequent occasions on which leads had to be changed, they would have to be dragged out and put in other places. When using a distributing-board the leads when once connected need never be disturbed, only the connecting wires between the two boards being altered, the special arrangement above described allowing this to be done with the greatest ease and regularity.

Since its installation in 1888, the Manchester system has worked very successfully. The whole of the connecting blocks, etc., were made by the Western Electric Company. Fig 171 gives a general view of the test-board and back of cross-connecting board, and also shows the testing instruments.

Subsidiary Distributing Board.—Many of the exchanges in America are provided with two distributing boards, one in the position described above, and a second at the opposite end of the switch-board. To this additional one the cables, after connecting up all the ordinary spring-jacks, are brought before connecting up the local spring-jacks. For the ordinary purpose of getting connection between subscribers by the multiple board, it does not matter how the 200 subscribers which the operators on any one table attend to are composed. They need not be in numerical order, as, when a call is made, the operator simply inserts a plug in the corresponding local jack to answer the call and connects the number asked for by plugging into one of the ordinary jacks, to which the subscribers *must* be connected in proper numerical order. The object of the second distributing board is to divide the specially busy numbers among the operators, so as to equalise their work.

Coleman & Jackson's Test-Board.—Figs. 172 and 173 show the arrangement of springs and lightning arresters used on this test-board, which is somewhat similar to

Fig. 171.

the Manchester form, except that the line springs C C are arranged on horizontal shelves, and the contact blocks D D are provided with other springs, F F, which press against the main springs and ensure a good con-

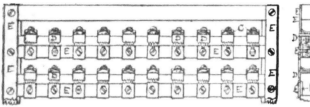

Fig. 172.—Scale ¼.

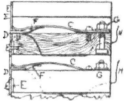

Fig. 173.—Scale ¼.

tact. When the test-shoe is inserted the two springs are separated. The line wires are connected to terminals G G, and the switch-board wires are soldered to wires H H, connected to the contact blocks. This board is in use in many exchanges, including Birmingham and Bradford, and serves its purpose well.

A neat form of test-board is shown in Figs. 174 and 175. For each line two brass pieces, A and B, are clamped to a base board, one of which overlaps the

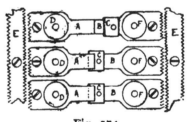

Fig. 174.

Fig. 175.—Scale ⅓.

other but does not touch it. Connection is made between the two by a sliding piece of brass, C, dove-tailed on to B, and furnished with a knob ; A, B, C form part of the circuit of the lines. On wishing to test the piece, C is drawn from under A, and a brass plug attached to the test set is inserted into holes D or F, according to which part of the line is to be tested.

The Power Generator.—This is simply a magneto generator mounted on a stand or base, and arranged to be driven by a machine of some kind, generally a water-motor. Bailey & Co.'s "Thirlmere" water-motors are

Fig. 176.—Scale ⅕.

very convenient for the purpose, the smallest, or No. o size, generally sufficing.

When the exchange is not large the ordinary size of generator will be sufficient to supply the current required, but special large-sized ones are made for centres where the demand upon them is considerable. In such cases it will often happen that ringing will be taking place over several lines at the same time, and as the lines vary very much in resistance, some, such as the trunk lines of high resistance, may get little current. To remedy this, it is necessary to keep the generator of a low resistance, but at the same time the E.M.F. must be kept up. To fulfil these requirements it is necessary to employ generators of larger size, so that a large number of turns of thick wire may be put on the armature.

Fig. 176 shows a form of generator much used, having a resistance of about 65 ohms. The current is collected by means of copper brushes, as in a dynamo machine.

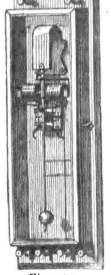

The generators are generally fixed in a closed case provided with a glass front, so as to keep out the dust and yet allow them to be visible to the attendant.

A Pole-changer is a very useful instrument for use in exchanges where power is not always available. By means of it the connections of a battery of about 10 cells are automatically changed by

Fig. 177.

the swinging of a pendulum, so that rapidly alternating currents can be sent to work magneto bells. It is made up of a polarised electro-magnet and armature, as show n in Fig. 177. The armature forms part of the pendulum the bobbin on which may be adjusted for different rates of vibration. The upper part of Fig. 178 shows the connections of the driving mechanism, *d* being a section o

O

the pendulum, and *h* a rigid contact block. The lower part of the figure shows the reversing arrangement, *e* being another section of the pendulum rod, and *r* another rigid piece.

A simpler form of pole-changer is shown in Fig. 179

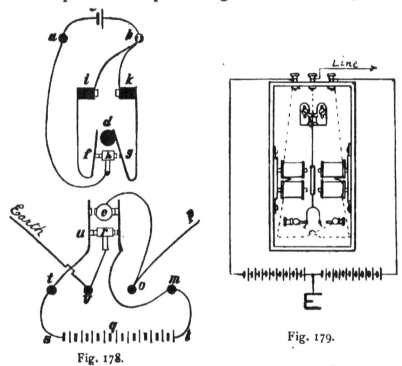

Fig. 178.   Fig. 179.

which also shows the connections. A double battery is required for this, as shown.

Much trouble is experienced in exchanges using generators and pole-changers, but especially the latter, owing to the inductive effects upon other wires when ringing. It is not so pronounced in the case of the generators, because the currents from these are more in the form of a regular wave, whilst with the latter they are sudden makes and breaks. Mr. Miller, of Dundee, has found that the connection of a condenser of one or two microfarads between the terminals of a pole-changer diminished the trouble very much, and in some cases suppressed it entirely.

Rough Testing Set.—The great majority of lines in a telephonic exchange are not more than half a mile in length, so that elaborate tests to determine the locality of faults are seldom necessary, and would usually result in waste of time, as the linesmen would generally have cleared the trouble in the time taken to locate by test. Many of the faults, such as contacts, do not require any test, and the telephone itself is such a delicate instrument that very frequently by its aid alone faults can be roughly located by an experienced test-clerk who has got used to the characteristic sounds given by the line under certain conditions.

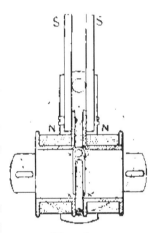

Fig. 180.

For faults which require rough tests the instruments required are : 1, a galvanometer ; 2, a battery of, say, 30 cells, so connected to a switch that a current from 1, 2, 4, 10, 20, and 30 cells may be obtained at will ; 3, a telephone set with magneto bell ; 4, switches and testing shoes.

The galvanometer should be one having a soft iron needle polarised by permanent magnets, as shown in Fig.180, as small magnetic needles are not reliable, the readings with the same current strength varying very much from time to time. The soft iron needle is of a tuning-fork shape, pivoted at the top, the same pivot carrying a pointer at the front, as shown in dotted lines.

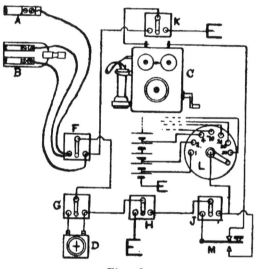

Fig. 181.

The instrument should be wound with two coils of wire, one of about 200 ohms resistance, provided with a $\frac{1}{10}$th shunt, and the other of about ·5 resistance.

Fig. 181 shows the connections of a convenient arrangement of the testing instruments :—A is the testing shoe for single lines; B for metallic circuit lines, C the telephone set and magneto; D galvanometer; F, G

H, J, K, two-way switches for altering the connections; L a rotary switch for altering the battery power; M a battery key.

By F connection can be made to one side or the other of the double test shoe; by G the galvo. can be put in or out of circuit; by H the shoe can be put directly to earth; by J a permanent current can be put to line; and by K the earth connection can be taken off the telephone set, and the latter included directly in the loop circuit.

Instruments for Electrical Measurements.—For such measurements as the conductivity, insulation resistance, or the static capacity of lines, more sensitive and accurate instruments are required. Every large centre where a number of long trunk lines are connected should be provided with a complete set of electrical testing instruments, comprising: 1, a Wheatstone bridge, with resistance box; 2, a reflecting galvanometer of high resistance, with shunts, lamp, and scale; 3, a standard condenser of about $\frac{1}{2}$ microfarad capacity; 4, well-insulated discharge key and battery reverser; 5, a tangent galvanometer.

Space will not allow of a description of these instruments and their use, for which the reader is referred to such books as Kemp's "Electrical Testing" or Professor Ayrton's "Practical Electricity."

CHAPTER XI.

OUTDOOR CONSTRUCTION.

Selection of Route.—In selecting a route along which to run a telephone line, care should be taken to avoid, as far as possible, longer spans than about 80 yards. Where only one or two wires are concerned in towns it is better not to erect poles, as they are expensive, and are in most cases objectionable to the neighbourhood. It is better to select strong chimneys, on the highest buildings, for the attachment of the insulator supports. The route chosen should be as straight as possible, in order to lessen the materials required, and to prevent excessive strain on the supports. In crossing over thoroughfares the wires must be at least 30 feet from the ground, in order to prevent accidents from fire-escapes. The wires should also cross the streets as near as possible at right angles, in order that they shall be seen as little as possible, and that if any should break there would be less danger of their falling into the street, to the danger of passers-by. The wires should not pass closely over chimneys, as the heated air very materially weakens the wire, especially during showery weather, when it is subjected to frequent alternations of heat and cold.

In the country, efforts should be made to keep clear of trees, the branches of which, if touching the wires, give rise to excessive leakage to earth. As the Government claim the sole right of running lines along the public roads in this country, recourse must be had to private property, and care must be taken that no damage is done to trees, fences, etc. Poles should be kept near the hedges, and should not be fixed in the middle of fields, or, at any rate, stays should never be used where cattle would be liable to be injured by them.

Railways should be crossed as little as possible, as the railway companies are very exacting in their conditions. In exposed situations advantage should be taken of any shelter from the prevailing winds.

Way-leaves or Easements.—Before the wire can be erected, it is necessary to obtain what are called way-leaves or easements, which are formal permissions from the owners of the property for the erection of poles or the attachment of wires to any building. To obtain these is frequently a very difficult matter, and one which requires much tact, judgment and perseverance. A nominal payment of 1s. per annum is usually made for the way-leave, but often a heavy payment is demanded and frequently has to be paid.

Wire.—Previously to about 1884 the wire used for running telephone lines was mostly of iron galvanised to protect it from rusting, which, however, it failed to do for long, especially in manufacturing districts, where its life was only about four or five years, and in many places much less. The size of wire used was generally No. 11, or 121 mils diameter, having a resistance of about 24 ohms to the mile.

Copper or bronze wire is now almost exclusively used, and for many reasons is much superior to iron. Copper is used for all trunk lines. As pointed out in Chapter I., it is one of the two best conductors, its resistance being only $\frac{1}{6}$th that of iron. This in itself would have ensured its adoption long ago, but that until a few years ago its mechanical properties were unequal to the requirements. By a process of what is called *hard-drawing* its mechanical strength has been raised from about 6·5 tons per square inch to about 29 tons, and it is now in every way suitable, being stronger than iron and equal in strength to mild steel. Copper corrodes but very slowly, in pure atmospheres hardly at all, so that the expense of renewal and maintenance is much reduced, especially in manufacturing districts.

In order to obtain an equal resistance, a wire of copper much thinner than of iron can be used. On this account copper wire does not attract so much attention on the part of the public, and, therefore, does not raise so much objection as iron wire.

The electrostatic capacity, being proportional to surface, is small in this thin copper wire. This is a very important matter in long-distance working. The magneto-induction, or *self-induction*, for the same form of wire is much less for copper than for iron, as shown by the experiments of Professor Hughes.   This also is a very strong point in favour of copper wire for long-distance working.   The supports for the lighter wire need not be as large or costly.   The old wire will command a good price as old copper.

Silicium-Bronze Wire.—All the advantages given above apply also to silicium-bronze wire,.so called not because silicium enters into the composition of the wire, but because its compounds are used as a flux in the manufacture of the alloy, which is composed of copper about 97 and tin about 3 parts in 100.

The properties of iron, steel, silicium-bronze, and hard-drawn copper wires of common sizes are given in the table below :—

	Gauge S. W. G.	Dia. in Mils.	Weight in lbs. per mile.	Res. per mile.	Ohm-Mile Constant	Tensile Strength in lbs.
Iron Wire	7½	170	400	12	4800	1069
	11	120	200	24	,,	535
	16	66	60	80	,,	160
Steel	16	66	60	103	6200	360
Silicium Bronze ...	16	66	64	30·5	1950	331
	18	48	38·5	50·1	,,	187
Hard-drawn Copper	11½	110	. 200	4·46	892	750
	14	79	100	8·92	,,	375
	16	66	70	12·74	,,	260

It will be seen that the great strength of the bronze wire is obtained at the expense of a high resistance, for which reason it is only used for short local wires.   Bronze wire loses its strength if soldered in the ordinary manner, as the heat necessary weakens the wire very materially. A mechanical joint or solder melting at a very low temperature should be used.

No 16 hard-drawn copper wire is used for local lines, No. 14 for trunk lines up to 50 miles, and the 11½ for long trunk lines.

No. 18 silicium-bronze wire is that generally used for local exchange lines.

Insulators.—As the wire used for telephone lines is mostly bare and must be supported at frequent intervals, it is necessary to provide special *insulators* to which the wire may be attached, and so prevent excessive leakage through the poles, which are not sufficiently good insulators in themselves. In addition to having high insulating qualities, the insulators must have sufficient strength to resist the strains to which they are subjected.

Material.—This has varied from the original goose-quill to earthenware, glass, ebonite and porcelain. White porcelain has given the best results, but well-glazed earthenware comes closely behind it, and has the merit of being cheaper. The principal requirement is that the material must not be porous, and must have a fine glazed surface which will not attract moisture.

Experience has shown that the leakage does not pass through the body of the insulator, but is altogether a matter of surface conduction by means of the films of dirt or moisture deposited on them.

Form.—In designing the form the object has been to make the surface over which the leakage must pass as long and narrow as possible consistent with strength, as the law of resistance is the same for films of moisture as for other substances. A dry portion of such surface must also be preserved in the wettest weather, which object is attained by making the insulator in the form of an inverted cup or cups.

Cordeaux's Screw Insulator.—This is probably the one which answers the above and certain other requirements to the fullest extent, for which reason it is mostly used for important telephone lines. Fig. 182 shows it partly in section and the galvanised iron bolt used in conjunction with it. It is a *double-shed* form of insulator, which means that it is in the form of an inverted double cup. *Single-shed* insulators have only one inverted cup. It will be seen that a great length of surface is opposed to the leakage between the wire (which is fastened in the groove) and the bolt. The screw arrangement shown allows of the insulator being taken apart from the bolt, when in position, for the purpose of cleaning out the inside or to change the position of the wires on the

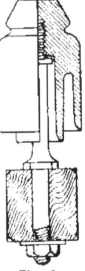

Fig. 182.
Scale ¼.

poles. An india-rubber ring, put over the screw, is used to allow for the difference in expansion by heat between the iron and the porcelain.

The wire is placed against one side of the groove and is then bound to the insulator by two lengths of 18's soft copper-wire, in the manner shown in Fig. 183, the binding wire being first wrapped round the line wire in order to prevent injury from the continual friction against the insulator. The wires are then whipped round the line from B to E, thence back to D; then from the *upper* side of the line wire round the neck of the insulator to the *under* side of the line at C, back over the first layer to B, and then finished off as a single layer to A.

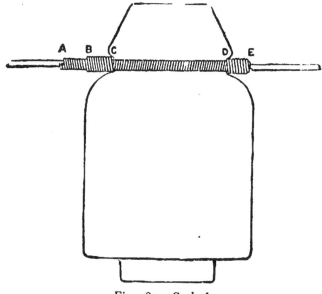

Fig. 183.—Scale ½.

In many circumstances the Cordeaux insulator is not suitable, such as when excessive strain is put on the supports by the wires going off at an angle. Also when the wires have to be *terminated* or *shackled off*, which means that the wires coming to and going from are fastened to the insulator independently of each other.

The *Langdon* Insulator, Fig. 184, is much used for such cases. It has three grooves, in each of which a wire may be terminated. The bolt cemented inside goes far above the grooves, so that if the insulator should break the wire cannot fall.

When circumstances require that additional security should be given, as when wires cross over important thoroughfares, they should always be terminated on each side. In many places all over-house wires are terminated.

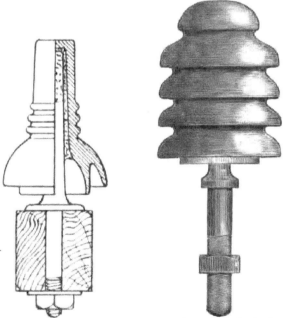

Fig. 184.—Scale ¼.   Fig. 185.—Scale ⅛.

Bennett's Insulator, Fig. 185.—This serves for terminating equally as well as the Langdon, and is superior to it in insulating powers and in other respects. It was specially designed to meet the various demands of telephone work by Mr. A. R. Bennett, and has been very extensively used and found to answer all requirements. It has four grooves in which wires may be terminated. If the wire is a light one, both terminations may be made in the top groove. The Bennett insulator is especially strong in resisting damage by stone throwing, usually a costly item in maintenance.

Double Shackle Insulator, Fig. 186.—This was almost universally used in England for over-house work until a

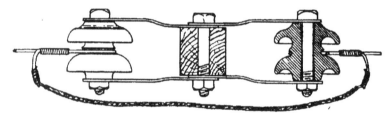

Fig. 186.—Scale ⅓.

few years ago, when attention was drawn to its very poor insulating power. For short lines this did not so much matter, but when long-distance telephoning became more extensive the electrical condition of the lines was required to be as perfect as possible, and the double shackles were discarded for the other forms of terminating insulators described, which give at least eight times better insulation. They are still used now and then, where great strength is absolutely necessary. Fig. 186 shows the method of terminating by their means.

Wooden Poles are used for nearly all but over-house

work for the support of the wires and insulators. They are generally round in section, but square ones are sometimes used to suit the taste of the proprietors of the land on which they are erected.

Creosoting.—Before use the poles should be subjected to some preservative process, many of which have been suggested and tried, but the only one which has given satisfaction is *creosoting*. This consists in forcing into the pores of the timber, when thoroughly seasoned, a quantity of creosote, an oily and antiseptic product of coal-tar. About 10 lbs. of creosote should be absorbed per cubic foot of timber. This process, if properly carried out, effectually protects the pole from *wet-rot*, which attacks unprotected poles at the ground line, where there are great alternations of temperature and moisture.

The poles used are mostly Norwegian or Swedish firs, felled in winter, when the sap is least plentiful. It is important that the natural butt of the tree should be attached.

An objection to creosoted poles is that they cannot be properly painted, as the oil oozes through. Their appearance is not therefore prepossessing.

Poles up to 65 or 70 feet in length can now be creosoted. When longer ones are required two poles should be *spliced* together, the top of one and the bottom of a smaller one being fitted together for some eight or ten feet, and then firmly clamped with iron bands, or wrappings of stay wire and bolts.

Poles are supplied in two sets, *light* and *stout*. The

first are for use on lines of not more than ten or twelve wires, and the latter for heavy lines above that number.

Erection of Poles.—The poles are planted in the ground about one-fifth of their length, except the longer ones, which need not be planted more than seven or eight feet in good solid ground.

In digging the hole an oblong space is first cut

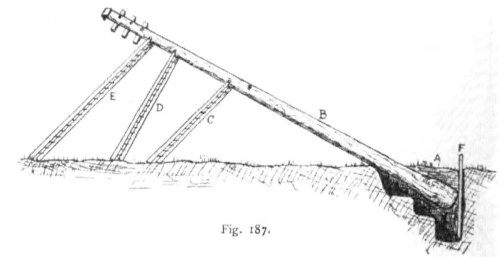

Fig. 187.

out about eighteen inches wide and four or five feet long, the longest side, if possible, being parallel with the line of the wires to be erected.   This space is then dug out in steps until the end where the pole is to rest has reached the proper depth.

The pole, with the arms attached, is then brought to the hole so that the butt lies over the deepest part.   It is next tilted up, and three or four strong ladders of different lengths are put under the top end.   By a couple of men or so at each ladder the pole is gradually raised a few inches each lift, the ladders being shifted in position one at a time, so as to keep them as near right angles to the pole as possible, to get the best effect and prevent slipping. This is further prevented by passing light ropes over the tops of the ladders after being fastened at the butt end of the pole.

Fig. 187 will give an idea of the method, A showing the form of the hole, B the pole, C, D, E the ladders, longer ones being used as the pole gets more upright, when it is also steadied by ropes. At F a board is shown at the end of the hole, which is to prevent the end of the pole digging into the soil and so impeding its erection. The sides of the hole prevent the pole falling over sideways. When the pole is upright the earth is filled in and well rammed or *punned* down with punning tools. This punning is very important, and should on no account be scamped, as the firmness of the pole depends altogether upon it.

When exceptionally large poles have to be raised, or poles have to be put in positions where ladders cannot be employed, a smaller pole is erected in some convenient position to be used as a *derrick*. Pulley blocks are attached to an arm at the top and to about the centre of the pole to be raised. By this means the latter pole can be swung round and its ends got in position, and then, by ladders and ropes called *sash-lines*, brought to the upright. Walls have often to be taken down before the work can be completed, and the skill of the men is often taxed in effecting the purpose.

Arming the Poles.—The arms used vary in length,

P

according to the number of wires they are to carry, whether two, four, or six wires on each, the most common lengths being 24, 42, and 54 inches respectively. The centre wires should not be less than 14 or 15 inches apart, in order to allow the men to get up between.

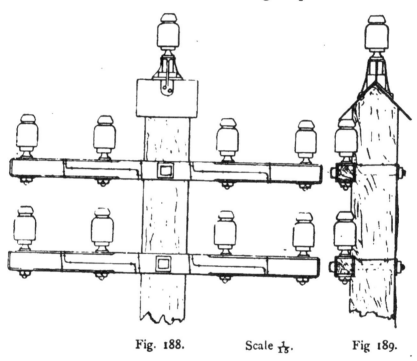

Fig. 188.   Scale $\frac{1}{15}$.   Fig 189.

The arms, which are usually of good sound oak, about $2\frac{1}{2}$ in. square in section, are fitted into grooves sawn on one side of the poles at about 12 inches apart, and are secured by a bolt which passes through pole and arm, as shown in Figs. 188 and 189, which also show the *pole roof* of galvanised iron fitted on the top of a pole and surmounted by a *saddle bracket*, into which the bolt of an insulator is fitted for carrying what is called the *cap* wire.

Earth Wiring.—Figs. 188 and 189 also show a wire which is run up from the bottom of the pole (where a coil of it is buried), and is stapled round the arms between each pair of insulators. This is intended to intercept any leakage which may occur over the insulators, and prevent its leaking into the adjoining wires carrying it off to earth instead.

The earth wire is sometimes connected to the bolts of the insulators but this is a mistake, as unless the wire makes good earth (which is very seldom the case) it helps the leakage from one wire to another, and causes excessive leakage to earth in wet weather.

Stays.—When the poles are exposed to heavy strains by the wires going off at an angle, *stays* or *guys* are used to prevent the pole going over in the direction of the strain. They are usually made up of seven No. 8

Fig. 190.

galvanised iron wires twisted together. One end of this is taken twice round the top part of the pole, the best position being midway between the top and bottom arms, so that it may act at the *resultant* point of the total pull of the wires on the pole.

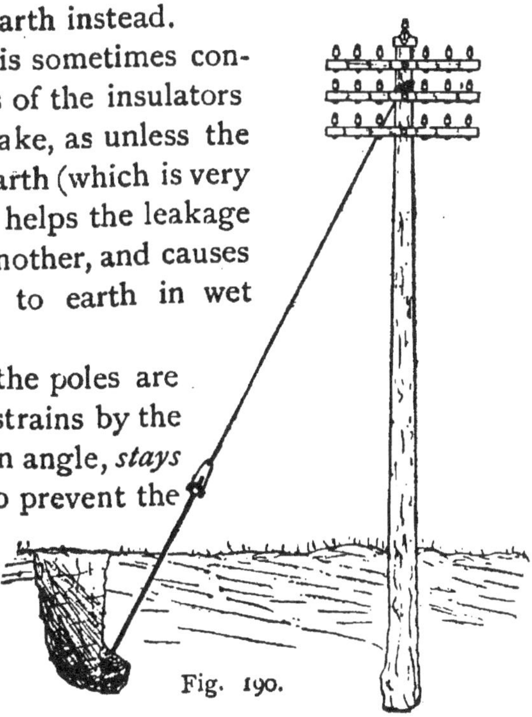

A hole is dug as far from the foot of the pole as is convenient, and in this hole a block of creosoted timber is placed, through which a long bolt, called a *stay-rod*, provided with a large *washer-plate*, is passed. The whole should be undercut, as shown in Fig. 190, so that the pull may be against solid earth. The top of the stay-rod is provided with a *swivel*, to which one end of the stay is attached. The swivel is so arranged that by turning a nut the stay can be tightened up.

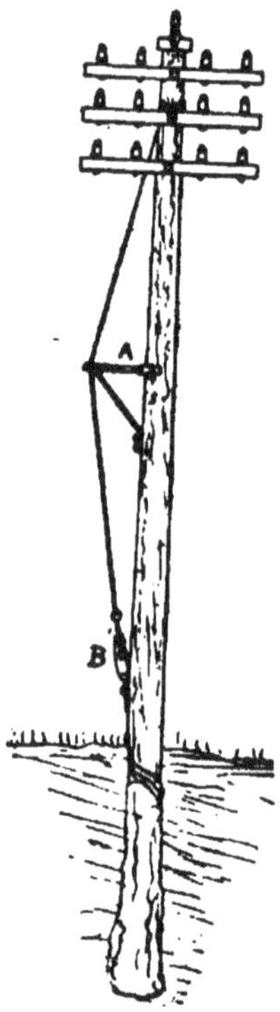

Sometimes two or three stays are required where the strain is excessive. Where the wires go off at nearly a right angle, it is better to fix two stays or two double stays, one being fixed in a line with one direction of the wires, and the second in a line with the other direction.

Struts.—In cases where stays cannot conveniently be fixed, struts are used, which consist of a rather shorter pole fixed at an angle to the main one and on the same side as the pull of the wires. A block of creosoted timber is attached to the foot of the strut by means of an iron strap, and this is buried about four feet in the ground. Struts should be avoided, if possible, as they are not nearly so satisfactory as stays.

Fig. 191.

In many cases it is better to *truss* the pole, as shown in Fig. 191, where an *outrigger*, A, is screwed to the pole on the opposite side to the pull, and a strong stay is passed through an eye in the end of the outrigger, and attached to a stay-rod and block buried near the foot of the pole, or the stay-wire may be secured to the bottom of the pole itself, being provided with a *stay-tightener* to strain the stay, as shown at B.

Over-house Work.—Chimney brackets, firmly nailed to the chimney, as shown in Fig. 192, are used to support the insulator of wires attached to chimneys or the corner of buildings. The bolt of the insulator is fixed in the socket at A. Care should be taken that the angle chosen is such that the pull of the wire is towards the chimney. If this cannot be managed, and the chimney shows any sign of weakness, an iron band should be fitted round it, or several loops of

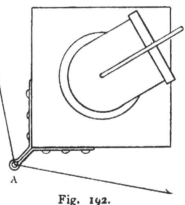

Fig. 192.

stay run round, so as to rest on the bracket and one or two courses of brickwork.

Complaint is often made of the noise caused by the vibration or *humming* of the wires attached to a building. A very simple method of preventing this is to wrap a long strip of lead, about ⅛ inch thick and ¼ inch wide, tightly round the wires, for about 8 inches on each side of the insulator. Another method is to terminate the wires on double shackles, the iron straps and bolts of which are replaced by tarred rope passed through the shackle cups. This forms what is called a *Sourdine.* Light and stranded wires do not give so much trouble in this respect.

Standards.—For carrying the wires of a telephonic

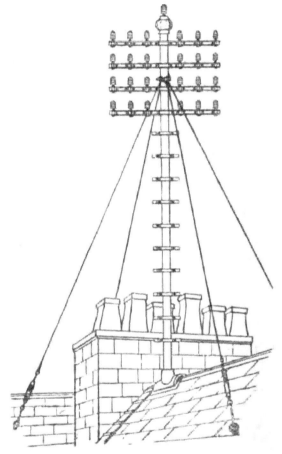

Fig. 193.—Scale $\frac{1}{40}$.

exchange, where the buildings are high, *standards* are used which are fixed on the roofs. Some managers prefer wood for these standards, and others iron. The latter have a neater appearance and are fast supplanting the wooden ones. The style which is now generally used in this country was designed some years ago by Mr. A. R. Bennett.

Fig. 193 shows one of these iron standards, and the method of fixing on the ridge of a building. The upright part is a wrought-iron tube of from $3\frac{1}{2}$ to $4\frac{1}{2}$ inches diameter, the bottom of which is tightly wedged in a socket formed in a cast-iron chair, made so as to fit over the ridge of the roof. Before being put in position, sheet lead and two or three thicknesses of roofing felt are fitted on the ridge.

Tubes for these standards are made 3, $3\frac{1}{2}$, 4, and $4\frac{1}{2}$ inches diameter, the metal being $\frac{1}{4}$ inch thick, so that the smaller sized ones fit into the next size above. The usual lengths are 15, 18, and 24 feet. Many standards are formed by two tubes, one fitted inside the other for a length of about 2 feet, and secured by two bolts passing through the tubes. Standards of 40 feet or more in length may thus be obtained.

Iron Arms.—Fig. 194 gives a view of one of the arms on a larger scale. They are formed of two lengths of channel iron, so shaped that when screwed together by the bolts shown they grip the tubes, and leave spaces for the bolts of six insulators. The arms thus formed are 5 feet long, $1\frac{1}{4}$ inch wide, and $1\frac{1}{2}$ inch deep. Fig. 195 gives a section to a scale of one-third.

Four wire arms are also made for use where heavy wires are used, or the number of wires is small.

Iron standards must be well stayed, in order to resist

the strains upon them.   For short ones it is usual to
attach four stays, as shown in Fig. 193, each provided
with stay-tighteners, and attached to wrought-iron *stay-eye
clips*, which are iron bands passed round and clamped on
to the strongest beams of the roofs, leaving an iron ring
projecting through the roof, to which the stays are

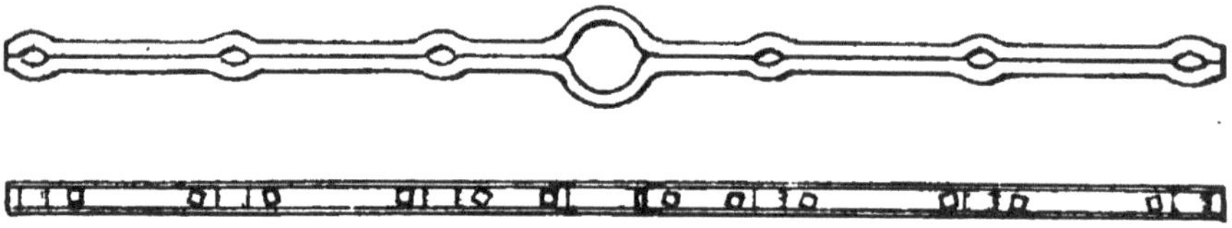

Fig. 194.—Scale $\frac{1}{16}$.

attached.   The roof at these points must be *flashed* with
sheet lead to prevent leakage of water.

If the standard is a long one, or is subjected to
specially severe strains, more stays are attached, some
being fixed at a lower point of the standard.
Two or more stays may be fixed to the same
eye-clip.   The staying of iron standards is very
important, and great care should be taken that
it is thoroughly well done.

Fig. 195.

Trussed Standard.—Where difficulty is experienced
in arranging sufficient stays, an arrangement like Fig.
196, also due to Mr. Bennett, may be adopted.   The
trussing is effected by four steel or iron rods, fastened
at their upper and lower ends by screws and nuts, by
means of which they can be strained over a cast-iron disc
fastened to the tube midway between the foot and the
lowest arm.   Fig. 197 gives details of A on a larger
scale, and Fig. 198 details of B and C.

Another method of fixing iron standards is to fit a block of timber about 6 feet long, and 8 or 9 inches square in section to the ridge of the roof. The tube is fitted into a hole bored in the block, which takes the place of the iron chair, and strengthens the roof by spreading the pressure over several principals.

Double, triple, and multiple standards are made up of two, three, or more upright tubes or combinations of tubes, connected together by specially long arms. On the principal routes in Glasgow five double tubes are thus connected by long arms, 32 wires being carried on each of the latter, 30 of these arms being fixed from top to bottom thus giving a carrying capacity of 960 wires.

The frontispiece to this book shows the square standard on the roof of the Mutual Telephone Company's Exchange in Manchester, formed of combinations of the tubes and arms braced together by iron rods and rings, making a very neat and strong structure.

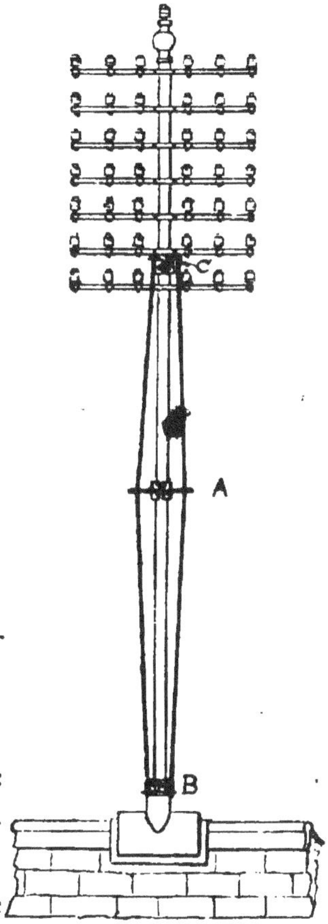

Fig. 196.—Scale $\frac{1}{75}$.

When *wooden standards* are used for over-house work they are generally square in section, and are taken through the roof and firmly bolted and braced to the timber work or to one of the walls of the building, through which

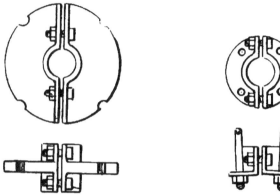

Fig. 197.—Scale $\frac{1}{12}$.   Fig. 198.—Scale $\frac{1}{12}$.

clips are passed and large wall-plates fixed so as to brace the standard firmly to the wall. Sometimes the

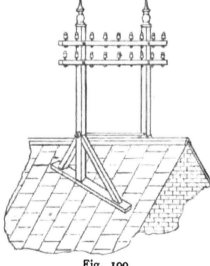

Fig. 199.

standard is fixed outside against a wall with clips and wall-plates inside. Stays may often be dispensed with for wooden standards.

Clayton Standards.— Objection is often raised to the standard passing through the roof, in which case a Clayton standard may be used, which is a wooden framework so constructed that it strides over the ridge as shown in Figs. 199 and 200.

It is braced by an iron rod as shown. These standards have the advantage that they can be made so that the arms cross the ridge of the roof at any angle. They should be well stayed to give stability.

Fig. 201 shows an arrangement of Mr. Bennett's by means of which two wire arms may be converted into

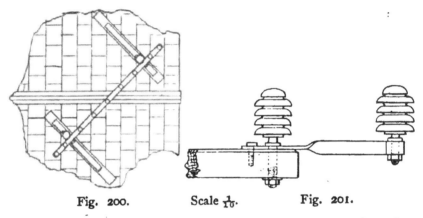

Fig. 200.   Scale $\frac{1}{16}$.   Fig. 201.

four wire arms, and four wire arms into six, the extending piece being of wrought-iron formed into a boss at one end.

Running the Wires.—The wire is supplied from the makers in coils of about 70 pounds in weight and 18 inches diameter. It should not be directly unwound from the coils, or it would be apt to get into kinks and twists. A kind of wheelbarrow, provided with a drum, on which the coil fits, is used, from which the wire may be unwound under tension.

On straight runs in the country the wires are terminated at about every sixth pole, being simply bound to the insulators of the intermediate poles. The terminating is done to prevent the running back if a span should break.

Dip or Sag.—The amount which a wire falls at the centre of the span when its points of suspension are at equal heights is called its *sag*. There will always be some sag, no matter how tightly the wire is stretched. In order not to strain the wire more than one-fourth of

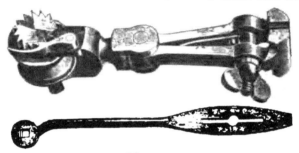

Fig. 202.

its breaking stress, the sag should be as given in the table below, (taken from Preece and Maier's book), for hard-drawn copper wire of 100 pounds to the mile.

100 LBS. HARD-DRAWN COPPER WIRE.

Span.	Low Winter Temp.		Ordinary Winter Temp.		Average Summer Temp.		High Summer Temp.	
Yards.	Sag. ft. in.	Stress. lbs.	Sag. ft. in.	Stress. lbs.	Sag. ft. in.	Stress. lbs.	Sag. ft. in.	Stress. lbs.
100	2 8	80	3 7	59	4 $3\frac{7}{8}$	49	4 $11\frac{1}{2}$	43
90	2 2	80	3 1	56	3 $9\frac{1}{2}$	46	4 $4\frac{5}{8}$	40
80	1 $8\frac{3}{8}$	80	2 $6\frac{7}{8}$	53	3 $2\frac{1}{4}$	$42\frac{1}{2}$	3 $8\frac{7}{8}$	36
70	1 $3\frac{5}{8}$	80	2 $1\frac{3}{4}$	49	2 $8\frac{5}{8}$	38	3 $2\frac{1}{2}$	33
60	$11\frac{5}{8}$	80	1 9	44	2 $3\frac{1}{8}$	34	2 $8\frac{1}{4}$	29
50	8	80	1 $4\frac{5}{8}$	39	1 10	29	2 $2\frac{3}{8}$	24

For other wire the sag should be the same, but the stress will be in proportion to the weight per mile, 200-pound wire producing double the stress given in the table. For different spans the sag should vary as the square of the length.

The wire is drawn up by being gripped by a *draw-vice*, Fig. 202, to the drum of which the wire, after being taken round the insulator, is attached. By using the key shown to turn the drum, the wire may be drawn to any degree of tightness, being held from running back by the ratchet and pawl until the wire is jointed.

Regulating.—One of the wires is then regulated for sag by the wire men, who use their judgment in regard to it. (They cannot be got to use the special dynamometers, provided with a Salter's spring and scale to show the tension, which are made for the purpose, the use of which should be much more satisfactory.) After

Fig. 203.

one wire is regulated the others are drawn up until they are parallel with it.

The wire, after bending round the insulator, is bound with a piece of No. 18 soft copper wire. The soldering of this and other joints must be done with a hot soldering bolt, and as quickly as possible, to prevent the heating and weakening of the wire.

In joining two lengths of wire together, the Britannia joint, Fig. 203, should be used. The figure is exaggerated in size.

Length of Spans.—The greater the number of wires carried by a line of poles, the shorter should be the distance between the poles, to give greater strength.

Snow often plays havoc with the wires under certain conditions by adhering to them until they become perhaps one or two inches thick, putting a great strain on the wires and the poles, especially if the wind is strong at the time.

For heavy lines of, say, 30 wires, the spans should be little over 50 yards, but may reach 80 yards for light lines.

The height of poles should be arranged so that the lowest wires will not be less than 20 feet from the ground, and over public roads not less than 25 or 30 feet.

When taller poles have to be used at special points of a route, the poles on each side should be also higher, so as to gradually raise the height of the line, for the sake of appearance and to save stress on the poles.

Heavy lines, even on straight routes should be stayed at every few poles, to give lateral strength to resist wind pressure.

Cables.—At a large telephonic exchange where the outside wires become crowded, and in many other cases, it is advisable to make use of cables consisting of a number of insulated wires twisted together and finally firmly bound and protected by an outside covering impervious to weather influences. The insulated wires of which a cable is composed are sometimes each encased in a covering of lead-foil, which is also connected to an outer covering of lead joined to earth. This effectually prevents cross-talk, but gives a large static capacity. Some cables, such as those of Glover & Co., are made up of No. 20 gauge wires, insulated with gutta-percha or indiarubber, covered with tape soaked in ozokerit, and then enclosed in an outer covering of lead, prepared tape, and a firm braided covering soaked in a bituminous compound. By using white coverings to some wires and black to others, and arranging them in a peculiar manner, it is possible to pick out any special wire without testing. An 84 wire cable of this class gives a static capacity of ·4 microfarads per mile.

The Fowler-Waring cables are very good for telephonic work, a paraffin compound being used for insulating the wires, giving a static capacity of about ·26 microfarads per mile. The Siemen's cables, made up in different ways, are also very good.

Some cables are intended specially for use with single wire systems and others for metallic circuit systems, the wires for the latter being twisted in pairs or fours, or sometimes eights, so as to get rid of speaking induction.

Other cables, such as those described in Chapter XIV., in which the protected wires are enclosed in a lead tube, are sometimes used for overhead work, but their great weight is much against their use for such purpose.

Cable Suspension.—Very few cables are strong enough in themselves to support their own weight, so that they are generally carried on strong *suspending wires*, which are often made of a stranded steel wire composed of seven No. 16 galvanised steel wires twisted together. Double shackles of extra strength are used to support the suspending wires, and the cable is supported at dis-

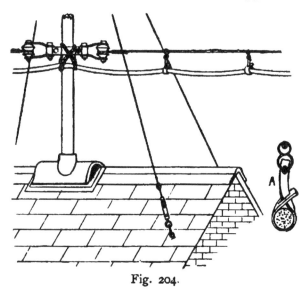

Fig. 204.

tances of every 3 or 4 feet by *suspenders*, which are either made up of short lengths of stiff wire, or, what is better, and has come much into use lately, by short pieces of raw hide attached to a hook or ring, which is threaded on the suspending wire, as shown in Fig. 204, which also shows the cowhide, etc., on a larger scale at A.

CHAPTER XII.

LONG-DISTANCE WORKING.

WHERE long trunk lines are concerned the conditions of working must be the best possible, in order that good articulation may result. All points that affect the good electrical condition of the circuit must be looked to.

The points for consideration come under two divisions:—1, Those in connection with the lines; and 2, those in connection with the instruments.

In regard to the latter, care must be taken that only good and firm contacts are made in switching from one line to another; that all joints included in the circuit shall be perfect; that there shall be no unnecessary shunts to earth; and, even more important than the above, that the apparatus included directly in the circuit shall oppose as little electro-magnetic inertia—also called *inductance*—as possible to the rapidly-alternating speaking currents.

The relative value of the inductance of different forms of apparatus used in telephony, as determined by

Q

Messrs. Ayrton & Perry's secohmmeter, is given in the following list:—

1 mile of round copper wire	=	1
1 do. do. soft iron wire	=	6
Ordinary telephone receiver	=	7 to 9
Siemen's receiver	=	14
Secondary wire of transmitter induction coil of res = 150 ohms.	=	26
Drop indicator, res = 9 ohms.	=	7
Do. do. without armature, res = 142 ohms.	=	77
Do. do. with armature	=	155
Electric bell (bobbins in series)	=	86
The same with bobbins joined in parallel	=	21
Electro-magnet, res = 260 ohms.	=	240

The list shows that the inductance of the electric bell coils joined up *in series* is four times that of the same coils joined in *parallel* or *multiple*. Electro-magnet coils that must be included directly in a speaking circuit should therefore be joined up in the latter manner. For the same winding of the coils this would result in weakening the magnetic power by one-half; but the latter may be restored by winding each coil to double its former resistance, and the inductance will still be reduced by one-half.

A copper wire equal to 6 or 8 times the resistance of the coils, joined up to the latter as a shunt, will considerably reduce the retarding effect, with but little weakening of the magnetic power.

· A condenser joined to the two ends of the magnet coils has also a similar effect.

The Line.—The principal trouble in regard to long trunk lines is due to the inductive action of one line upon others running side by side with it. After running thus for two or three miles, the induction enables nearly all that is said on one line to be heard on the others, and the overhearing gets more pronounced the longer the lines run together.

The overhearing may be also due to the leakage of the electric currents from one line to the others, and this is often the main cause of the trouble. Shackle cup insulators, defective pole earth-wiring, and bad earths for the pole earth wires, are the main causes of this leakage.

The trouble is a serious one, as the overhearing of a firm's messages by another firm in the same line of business is very objectionable.

Besides inductive voices, other noises are heard on single-wire lines which interfere with speaking and are irritable to those who use the lines. The noises are of several kinds, such as bubbling, crackling, hissing, whistling, and rasping sounds. They appear to be mostly caused by the swaying of the wires generating induced currents by cutting through the lines of force due to the earth's magnetic action; by the conditions of temperature at different points along the lines; by earth currents, and by induction from telegraphic and sometimes electric light circuits.

The only method of getting rid of these noises and

the speaking induction is by dispensing with the earth as the return part of the circuit, and using metallic or loop circuits. It is necessary that the two wires of a metallic circuit, be so arranged that they are equally exposed to any outside inductive influence, such as from telegraphic or other telephonic wires.

Two methods are adopted in practice to attain this object of equidistance. One called the *twist* system, by which the two wires of the line are continually twisted round each other and round a common axis, and the *cross* system, in which the wires are run straight and parallel to the outside wires, but their positions are reversed at certain points, so that the left-hand wire goes to the right, and *vice versâ*. The number of crossings having to be such as to make both wires (taking their whole length) the same average distance from other lines running near.

The *twist* system was suggested by Professor Hughes, and was first arranged in practice between Manchester and Oldham by Mr. J. E. Heys, for the late Mr. Charles Moseley. Figs. 205 and 206 show the plans adopted. In Fig. 205 a telegraph wire is shown on one end of the arms, and a twist telephone loop circuit on the other end. The wires of the latter make a complete revolution round each other in every four spans of the route, the position at every fourth pole being the same. The induced currents in both the loop-line wires, caused by the starting of a current in the telegraph line being in the same direction and of equal strength, will meet and neutralise each other at the ends of the loop. In order that the neutralisation may take place in the telephones at each end, it is necessary that the resistance of each branch of the loop shall be equal or *balanced*. If the balance is disturbed, overhearing and noises will ensue. Fig. 206 shows two loop circuits run on the same poles, two arms of each being utilised. Four circuits may be run on two longer arms, as shown diagrammatically in

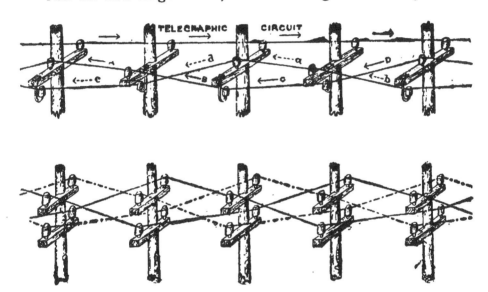

Figs. 205 and 206.

Fig. 207, two circuits on each side of the poles being twisted together. The loop wires are 1 and 3, 2 and 4, 5 and 7, and 6 and 8, and the diagram shows the position on five successive poles.

Although the twist system answers its purpose perfectly, there are certain drawbacks in connection with it. Wires run on the twist are more liable to faults, especially contacts, and much more difficulty is experienced in tracing the faults, as it is not easy for the linemen when walking along the route to see when lines are in contact, as even when the wires are in good order they appear to cross each other. The wires are more difficult to regulate, and from a distance always look as though they were out of regulation.

Experience has shown that on most telephone routes very few turns or crossings of the loop wires are necessary to produce silence. Three or four, or even less turns made evenly along the route are in most cases

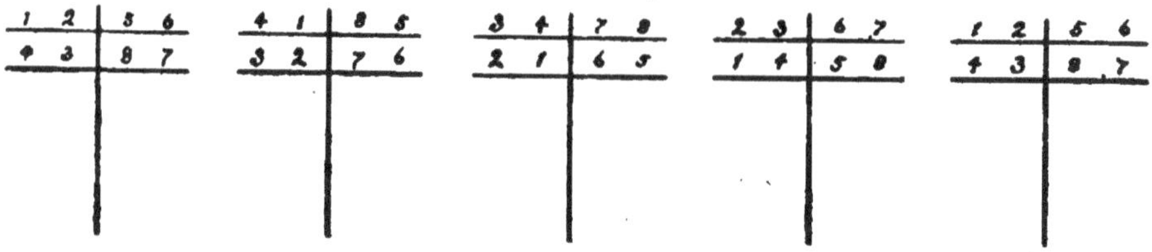

Fig. 207.

sufficient to ensure silence in a 20-mile line. In many cases one half turn is sufficient. On the twist system, as described above, seven or eight turns are made per mile, or about 140 turns in a 20-mile line. This amount of twist is far more than is necessary.

The Cross System.—This method has been used since 1884 on the trunk lines, which were under the control of Mr. A. R. Bennett, in Scotland, and the plan is generally followed on the Continent and in America.

The wires run straight on the poles, just as ordinary single lines, but at certain points the wires are terminated on double arms and insulators, or on double brackets and insulators, as shown in Fig. 208, which also shows the method of crossing adopted by Mr. Bennett, stranded wires, consisting of three or four pieces of the copper line wire, being twisted together, one of the two crossing pieces being straight, and the other arched under or over the straight one. These stiff connections cannot easily be brought into contact by birds, etc.

Two or three loop lines may be run on the same arm,

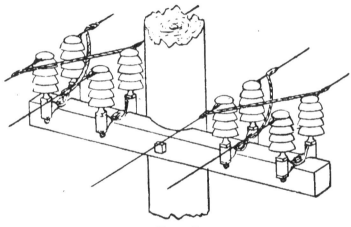

Fig. 208.

all such loops having their crossings made at the same poles. The same number of loops may be run on the next arm, but, in order to neutralise all induction, it is necessary that the crossings shall be made midway between the crossings on the upper arm, and a similar relation must exist between the crossings on the second and third arms. Fig. 209 will explain this :— A representing one pair of loop wires on the top arm, with one crossing ; B, a loop line on the second arm, with two crossings midway between that of A ; and C, a loop on the third arm with four crossings. Loops on a fourth arm would require eight crossings, on a fifth arm 16 crossings, and so on. The number of crossings on a route may be twice or four times as many as those given above.

The plan of crossings given is not the only one which may be adopted, but appears to be the one which requires the least number of crossings.

The system appears to answer its purpose perfectly well, and has none of the drawbacks mentioned in regard

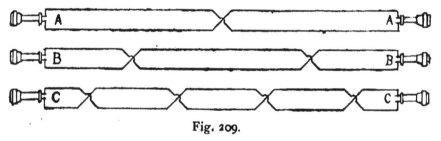

Fig. 209.

to the twist system. A careful consideration of the points of crossing is necessary, the men being instructed on what numbered poles the wires are to be crossed.

Translators.—The fact that most telephonic exchanges were worked by single lines and earth circuits when metallic circuit trunk lines were first adopted gave rise to a difficulty in connecting the two kinds of circuits together without interfering with the efficacy of the loop lines. An earth connection made to the latter at any point at once destroys its quietude, so that it was not possible to connect the single lines direct to the double lines. A way out of this difficulty was found by Mr. A. R

Bennett, by his invention of the *translator* or *repeater*, which is an induction coil, the primary and secondary wires of which are equal, or nearly equal, in resistance, and are wound on the bobbin together.

A translator is used at each end of the loop line, one of its coils being joined direct to the loop lines, the other coil being joined one end to earth, and the other to the switch-board, for connection with the subscriber's lines. Fig. 210 shows the connection adopted by Mr. Bennett :—T and T' are the two translators ; s

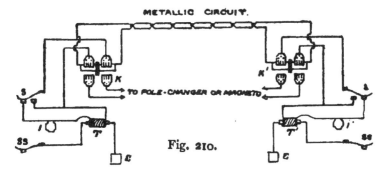

Fig. 210.

and s' two spring-jacks inserted in the loops, so that two such loop lines may be connected together, directly, by means of double cords and double plugs or shoes, one part of the plug connecting to the spring, and another part to the back contact shown. By the use of s and s' the repeaters are cut out when two loops are joined together. I and I' are two drops included in the loop circuit for calling purposes ; K and K' two double table switches, like the Dewar, for ringing purposes. When the lever is pulled down the two loop

wires are connected directly to the batteries or generator. SS and SS.' are two spring-jacks by which the
subscribers' lines are connected.

It has been found that each repeater reduced the
intensity of the sound by 30 or 40 per cent., and as
the sound passes through two repeaters, evidently the
received sound is much reduced in intensity. When
iron wire was used for the line wires this reduction was
felt very seriously, but now that copper line wires are
used the loss can in most cases be spared, a good
margin of strength being left, so that the loss is not so
much noticed. Complete metallic circuits, used for both
subscribers' and trunk lines, enabling the translators to
be discarded, will give a much more satisfactory service,
and will no doubt be universally adopted before long.

Translators have been recently introduced, the soft
iron cores of which are constructed of thin wires, about
$2\frac{1}{2}$ times the length of the bobbin, round which they
are bent (after the coils are wound on) until they
overlap on the outside, so that they form a complete
magnetic circuit, and completely envelope the coils.
This form, called the Liverpool repeater, gives improved
results in speaking, and has the further advantage that
ringing can be repeated, so that subscribers are able
to ring through to each other. This, however, is seldom
advisable, as the ring-off signal is given by so doing.
An indicator drop for signalling is necessary with this
translator, as with the older form, but is generally included in the *home* circuit instead of the loop. It is
advisable to get rid of this drop and its injurious

effect on the speaking. With this object in view, a translator was invented by Messrs. Coleman and Jackson, in which the drop forms part of the repeater itself. Fig. 211 gives a view of the instrument. The repeater coils, with core, are enclosed in a soft iron cylinder,

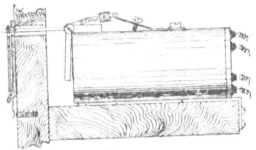

Fig. 211.

to the open end of which one end of the armature is pivoted, the latter having a lever attached, a hook on the end of which supports the drop fixed in front. The instrument serves its purpose very well both for ringing and speaking.

Switch-Room Arrangements.—Trunk lines, as a rule, require more attention on the part of operators than the ordinary local subscribers' lines, by reason of the greater difficulty of speaking and being so constantly engaged, and also because the connections have to pass through at least two switch-rooms, and two operators at least are concerned in making the connections.

Single-wire trunk lines are being fast superseded by metallic circuits, for the working of which special apparatus is employed.

Where only a few trunk lines are concerned—say up

to 8 or 10—they may be worked with the ordinary subscribers' lines and by the same operators. If they are single lines this can be done without alteration of the general arrangement, the trunk lines simply taking the place of an ordinary line. Where the number of trunk lines is more than 10, it is generally better to work

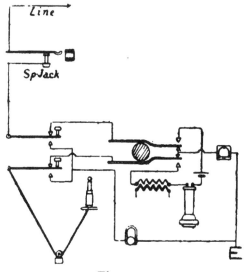

Fig. 212.

them on separate tables, by special operators who can devote all their attention to them.

A good and quick method of working single-line trunks is by means of the single-cord system, each trunk line ending in a cord and plug, in circuit with which is provided a Dewar or other table-switch and ringing keys, as shown in Fig. 212. The drop should be of high resistance if the line is a long one, say, from 200 to 400 ohms, and should preferably be a box or ironclad drop, so as to have a good amount of inductance, as it is joined in shunt when the line is connected to another one. The operator's set is provided with a test cell for multiple testing.

Fig. 213 is a sketch of the connections for working a

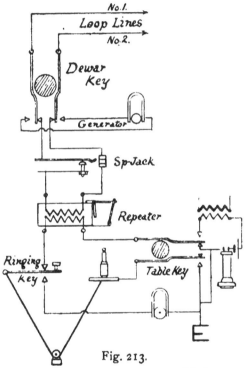

Fig. 213.

Coleman-Jackson translator. It will be seen that the local circuit of the translator is not complete when the line is not in use. This arrangement is adopted because the drop is much more sensitive under such circumstances. A test cell for multiple testing is shown also in Fig. 213.

The connections to the Liverpool pattern repeater are similar to Fig. 210, but the signal drop is included in the local circuit instead of in the loop circuit.

Limiting Distance of Speech.—Mr. Preece has shown that the length of line through which it is possible to speak is dependent upon (1) The total resistance of the circuit; (2) the total electro-static capacity; (3) the electro-magnetic inertia of the circuit. As copper is now universally employed for long-distance lines, the latter may be neglected, except in regard to the instruments. When the product of the total resistance and the total capacity of the circuit (or what is called the K. R.) is not greater than 15,000 on overhead lines and 12,000 for underground or submarine circuits, Mr. Preece states that it is just possible to speak, but the product should only amount to two-thirds of the above figures to ensure good results.

Single-line earth circuits and metallic circuits have the same limiting length, as although the resistance of the latter is double that of the former, the total capacity is only one-half that of the single line or only one-quarter per mile of wire. The difference in regard to overhead and cable lines is owing to the fact that the leakage on the former enables the static charges to escape easier to earth.

The capacity of cables is much greater than of overhead lines (over 20 times greater), and therefore the limiting distance is soon reached, for which reason open wires should be used for trunk lines where possible.

The table below gives the limiting distance of speech

through a few sizes of overhead copper wire and two sizes of cables. For the latter the top numbers represent the gauge of wire, and the lower numbers the gauge of its covering of gutta-percha.

Gauge.	Diameter in mils.	Res. in ohms. per mile.	Capacity per mile in microfarads.	Limiting distance of speech.	Distance at which speech is easy.
16	65	13	·008	380	316 miles
14	83	8·4	·0103	427	350 ,,
12½	100	5·7	·0124	461	376 ,,
16/4	65	13	·240	62	50 ,,
14/4	83	8·4	·290	70	56 ,,

The London and Paris Telephone Line is the most striking instance of long-distance telephony in connection with this country. A few details will therefore be of interest.

The submarine cable is laid between St. Margaret's Bay, near Dover, and Sangatte, in France, and is about 21 knots, or 24¼ miles, long. The conductors in the cable are four in number, each composed of seven copper wires, and weighing 160 lbs. per knot, with a resistance of 7½ ohms. Each conductor is insulated with three alternate layers of Chatterton's compound and gutta-percha, the total weight of each core being 460 lbs. The capacity per knot is about ·3 microfarad. Fig. 214 gives a full-sized section of the cable, showing how the four conductors are arranged. The latter form part of two looped circuits, opposite or diagonal wires forming a pair. They twist round each other so as to guard against outside inductive influences. Over the four conductors tanned hemp is wrapped. Outside this is a spiral protective sheathing of 16 galvanised iron wires, the whole being coated with mineral pitch and sand.

The land lines in England are about 84·5 miles long, and consist of four wires, each weighing 400 lbs. per mile, and giving a resistance of 2·2 ohms per mile. The lines are run on the twist system, to prevent induction, on poles 70 yards apart.

On the French side only two wires for one circuit are

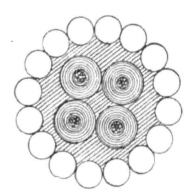

Fig. 214.

run, each weighing 600 lbs. to the mile, and of a length of 204 miles.

The K.R., or product of the total resistance into the total capacity of the one complete double circuit, is given as 7,359, with which speech should be good.

The instrument used at the London end is the Gower Bell, and at the Paris end the D'Arsonval receiver with the Roulez transmitter. Speaking is said to be excellent, although the total length of line is 311 miles.

CHAPTER XIII.

FAULTS AND THEIR LOCALISATION.

WITH the best class of instruments faults occur at times which interfere with, or altogether upset, the working of a station or stations. It pays to get instruments of the best class made by firms of high reputation, as the maintenance of such instruments is much less costly than that of cheaper ones.

In telephonic exchanges tests are made by the operators to each subscriber every morning of both ringing and speaking, and a list of those numbers found defective in any way is made out for further tests and rectification by the fault inspectors. Complaints of other defects are received during the day from the subscribers themselves, or from the renters of private instruments.

The most common descriptions of faults are such as: —wires in contact, can ring but cannot speak, cannot ring, cutting off whilst speaking, cannot get attention.

Such faults, with the exception of those in connection with private lines, are first reported to the test-clerk in

R

the test-room, who, with his instruments, endeavours to find out something more definite in regard to them, so as to guide the fault inspectors in tracing the cause, and to determine whether any faults exist at the switch-room end of the line. The faults, which are not in the switch-room, are reported to the instrument fault inspectors, with the exception of those which are obviously line faults, such as contacts between wires, when ringing or speaking on one of the wires is received on the others. The cause of the latter fault can only be in the switch-room or on the lines, except in very rare cases where the earth connections of two or more subscribers are obtained from the same water pipe, which has become defective from some cause or other.

When the fault inspector arrives at the subscriber's office, unless he is quite sure of the nature of the fault, he should make a few inquiries from the person who uses the instrument before he touches it. A few judicious questions will often throw much light on the nature of the fault, and as to in what part of the instrument the defect will most likely be found, whether in the bell part of the circuit, the speaking part, or in the local microphone circuit. For example, if the subscriber says *he can hear* from the other end perfectly, but *they cannot hear him* at all, it will be evident that the local microphone circuit must be faulty, or the secondary wire of the induction coil is short circuited. If he says *his bell rings*, but he *can neither hear nor be heard*, the speaking circuit must be looked to. If the instrument is a magneto, and *his own bell does not ring* when he turns the handle, the fault may be a disconnection in the bell part of the circuit, or somewhere outside, or the generator or bell is short circuited.

Before touching anything the inspector should make a careful examination of the parts affected, This will often disclose the cause of the trouble in a broken wire, a wire out of a terminal, or, perhaps, some bare part of wire touching another wire or terminal, or the earth connection may be severed or loose. If nothing is disclosed by this survey, and the last description of fault is indicated, the first thing to do is to connect the line and earth terminals of the switch-bell by means of a wire or other conductor, and try if the bell rings on turning the generator. If it does, the bell and generator will be all right, and the fault must be a disconnection in the earth or line circuit. If the bell does not ring, the fault must reside somewhere in it, and if it is further ascertained that the bell rings from the other end, the generator must be faulty, being either short circuited or disconnected between the automatic shunt points, and should be taken out and tested with a galvanometer and cell as to whether it shows a break or a very low resistance.

The subscriber may not know whether his bell rings or not. In which case it will be advisable to test the generator by connecting the galvanometer to the pole-piece, and to the spring which bears on the insulated pin at the end of the armature pivot, at the same time making a break in the bell circuit. By now turning the handle slowly, it will be evident if the generator is perfect by the deflections obtained. If the deflections are satisfactory, the bell must be looked to and tested for break or short circuit by the galvo and a cell.

If *ringing is all right* between the stations, but *speaking is not heard either way*, it will be evident that the secondary speaking circuit is defective. The receiver may be short-circuited or disconnected. A frequent cause of these faults is found in the connection of the flexible cord. Too much conductor is bared, and these bared parts get together, or the terminals work loose, and one of the conductors is pulled out. If this is not the faulty part, the switch hook contact should be cleaned, and if this does not remedy the trouble, the different parts of the circuit should be short-circuited one after the other, until the working of the instrument is restored.

If the subscriber *can hear but cannot be heard*, the local microphone circuit is affected. The defect may be caused by a bad cell, a dirty local spring contact, the latter being bent and failing to make a contact, a break or short circuit in some other part of the primary circuit or in the secondary wire of the induction coil. If a close inspection does not disclose the cause, and the battery cell is proved to be in good order by testing with a galvo, the different parts of the circuit should be tested by means of a length of wire, gradually by its means bridging over successive parts of the circuit until a sound is heard in the receiver, when the transmitter is blown upon. The break will then, as before, reside in the part last bridged over.

A good method of proceeding, if nothing definite can be learnt in regard to the fault, is, after looking over all the outside connections, to quietly take the receiver from the hook and put it to the ear. If the ordinary inductive noises are heard, it may usually be concluded that the secondary speaking circuit and the line wire at that end are all right, except that the secondary coil may be short-circuited, which, however, seldom happens. If now, on blowing into the transmitter a characteristic noise is heard in the receiver, it will be known that the speaking parts of the instrument are right. If the noise is heard on blowing, but the inductive noises are absent, the secondary circuit may be short-circuited or getting earth. If the disconnecting of the line wire from the line terminal of the instrument prevents the noise being heard, it will show that the instrument part of the speaking circuit is not at fault ; but to make sure that it is not in the leading wires, the line should be cut where it goes through the window, if there is the least suspicion that the trouble may be caused by staples, etc. If the noise, on blowing, does not disappear on disconnecting the line, the fault must reside in the instrument, and breaks must be made in the circuit and a battery cell and galvo used to find out which parts that ought to be separate are connected together, looking especially after points where wires cross each other. Screws or tacks used to fasten portions of the instrument often cause trouble by coming into contact with the connecting wires behind.

If the noise, on blowing, is faint, a fault may reside in

the transmitter or cell, or in the receiver, which should be examined by taking off the cap to see if there is any loose dirt in the bobbin recess, which might get between the pole-pieces of the magnet and the diaphragm, and weaken its vibration. This dirt is a very frequent source of trouble, and is one of the first things to look for in inspecting an instrument.

By the method of bridging over the connections when a break occurs, and of disconnecting and testing with a cell and galvo for a short circuit or earth, faults can, as a rule, be very soon located, and the necessary repairs are then a comparatively easy task, which, however, sometimes requires the changing of part of the instrument. Receivers, diaphragms, cords, zincs, and battery salts should be carried by the inspectors. The principal tools required by the latter are a small pair of cutting pliers, tweezers, a medium-sized and a small screw-driver, a pad handle with loose bradawls, gimlets, etc.

Intermittent Faults.—The faults spoken of above may be called *lasting* or *complete* faults, which exist continuously until rectified. The faults which often give far more trouble to locate are those which come on now and then and last but a short period, the instrument working in the intervals perfectly well. Such faults are often very difficult to discover, as there is nothing definite to work upon. The chief thing is to make inquiries under what circumstances the fault is observed, and how it affects the working, and from the answers obtained form some conclusion as to what part the i ͏   nent or line is affected. After which a close search for loose contacts, bad joints, broken wires, etc., must be made. The telephone cord frequently causes intermittent faults by the tinsel conductors becoming broken, or by part of the tinsel of one conductor piercing through the worsted covering and coming into contact with the other conductor causing a short circuit. This fault may usually be detected by putting the receiver to the ear and then continuously blowing on the transmitter, whilst with the other hand the cord is pulled, twisted and moved in different ways. If the fault is in the cord, this movement will cause the noise of blowing to chop off every now and then.

Those intermittent faults which occur on windy days may be put down to the line, as they are most likely due to a loose joint in the wire, a broken conductor in the leading wires, or caused by the wire itself swinging against some earth connection.

Two inspectors are often required to locate a fault of this kind, one at each end of the line.

Most Common Faults.—Many of the defects which crop up in connection with instruments have already been mentioned. Below will be found the most common faults which occur.

RECEIVERS.—*Cores too near diaphragm*, not allowing sufficient space for vibration. This is often caused by the receiver being dropped. It can be remedied in the Bell receiver by carefully knocking back with a hammer.

Diaphragm buckled, often caused by users poking pencils at it. A new one is often required may.

Dirt between Cores and Diaphragm.—Already referred to.

Bad soldered connection between the terminals and the wires leading to the coils, causing an intermittent fault. This may be detected by pressing in a certain direction on the terminals whilst listening and blowing on the transmitter or connecting to a battery.

Loose Bobbins.—Weak Magnet.—

TRANSMITTERS.—

The Blake.—Bad connections across hinges owing to rust and dirt. The safety springs should be bent well out, and the surface against which they press well cleaned.

Bad Soldered Connections.—

Carbon button pitted, by the users knocking against the front of the case or the diaphragm. A new button is often required, but sometimes the consequent faintness may be remedied by turning the button so that the platinum pellet bears on a fresh surface.

Diaphragm rusted, preventing its free vibration.

Rubbing a soft black-lead pencil over the surface of a carbon-button will often improve its working, as does also the drawing of a piece of notepaper between the contacts, which clears out dust and dirt.

PENCIL MICROPHONES.

Dirt in contact holes of carbon blocks, causing bad contacts and faintness. Pencils should be taken out and the holes cleared.

Bad wire connections, through faulty soldering or loose terminals.

GRANULATED CARBON TRANSMITTERS.

Damaged Diaphragms.—Being very thin, these are very liable to get punctured or cracked, thus allowing the granules to escape.

Faulty connections to carbon or platinum often occur.

MAGNETO BELLS.

Driving Gear Slipping.—This does not often occur with toothed gearing, but was a frequent source of trouble with friction driving gear.

Short circuits are sometimes caused by particles of brass ground off defective driving gear.

Telephone lever sticking and not making proper contact for speaking when receiver is removed. Spring should be strengthened and the lever taken off and pivot cleaned and rubbed with black-lead, as also any springs which bear upon it. No oil should be used on lever, as it will attract dust, thicken, and spoil the connection. Black-lead is much more satisfactory to use as a lubricator than oil in these cases.

Bad contacts on lever can be cured by scraping and rubbing with black-lead, as above.

Weak-polarising magnet should be replaced.

Gongs out of adjustment.

Lightning arrester plates short circuited, caused, perhaps, by loose nails, pins, etc., lying across.

BATTERY SWITCH-BELLS.

Bad Contact on Telephone Lever.—See above.

Faulty contacts on local contact springs caused by dust.

Trembler bell contact faulty through dust, causing a break in ringing circuit.

Residual magnetism, causing a break by attracting the armature and keeping the spring from the contact pin.

Faulty contact against back stop of ringing key.

BATTERIES.

Cracked cell, allowing the solution to run away.

Corroded, loose or dirty terminals or wires.

Faulty connection of wire to zinc rod.

Faulty connection between lead cap and carbon.

Exhausted solution, shown by crystals forming on zinc and porous pot.

Zinc rod consumed.

SWITCH-ROOM FAULTS.

Indicators sticking, owing to rusted pivots preventing armature moving, or to the shutters being too upright, so that they do not fall over when released. A little bending over will generally remedy the latter fault.

Bad contacts in spring-jacks, caused by dust. By means of a thin steel spring, provided with a handle and roughened by being cross-filed with a coarse file, the contacts in the jacks may be cleaned from the front of the table.

Bad joints, due to defective soldering.

Dust on the back contacts of ringing keys.

For locating faults on the W. E. Co.'s multiple board, an ebonite spring-jack plug is used to lift up the springs from their contacts without connecting them to the test-wire. By doing this on successive tables, and testing from the test-room, an earth or contact can be traced to a certain part of the board.

LINE FAULTS.—When faults are traced to the line

they are handed over to the *Linesmen*, whose duty it is
to find the cause and remedy it, and who should be
perfectly familiar with the various routes and the wires
upon them.

Line faults come under three principal headings :
1. *Contacts* between different lines ; 2, *Earth Faults*,
caused by wires coming into contact with some conductor connected to earth through more or less resistance ; 3, *Breaks*, either total or partial, caused by
bad joints or a fracture in the line or leaders at some
point.

1. In tracing contacts it is generally possible to find
out what wires are in contact, and, knowing this, the
linesmen can often walk at once to the point, as they may
know that the lines can only come together at one
point where their routes meet.

When the position cannot be so ascertained, a linesman will walk over the route of one of the lines, or
both, if they run together, and carefully scrutinize the
wires as he goes along. By so doing he will probably
come to the seat of the trouble. If the contact cannot
be found in this way, it becomes necessary to disconnect
one of the wires at some point, and then make a test
from the other end to discover if the contact has dis-.
appeared. If it has, the contact must be further away
from the testing station, and, the wire being again
joined up, other breaks are made further along, until
the lineman arrives at a point where the contact does
not disappear. The fault will then lie between the two
last disconnections. On long trunk lines test-boxes

are fixed along the route, into which the lines are led by G.P. covered wires, and attached to double terminals, so that tests may be easily made.

2. *Earth Faults.*—The procedure followed in tracing an earth fault is much the same as for a contact.

3. *Breaks.*—If a line is broken down, the linesman walks over the route until he comes to the broken span. On long lines, and when the fault is a difficult one to find, an earthed battery is connected to one end of the broken line, and the linesman every now and then connects the faulty line to earth through his galvo, and notes if he gets an indication of the current on the line. When he has passed the break the deflection will not be obtained. If an earth connection is not available, another wire may be used in place.

For *partial breaks* when the wire shows a very high resistance, the same procedure may be followed. A much weakened deflection will then be obtained when the fault is passed.

Intermittent line faults are a source of great trouble in locating, as in the case of similar instrument faults.

The linesmen should be provided with a portable telephone set, with either a battery of small dry cells or a small magneto bell for calling up the switch-room or test-room, but as these instruments cannot be made very light, and the men have often to walk long distances, the signalling is sometimes dispensed with, only light receivers being carried, appointments being made with the test-clerk to speak on the wire at certain times.

Morning Tests of Trunk Lines.—Special tests are

made every working morning of all the important trunk lines of a telephonic exchange. They are begun at 6 a.m., in order that the faulty lines may be rectified as far as possible before the general business hours commence. The tests made are rough insulation tests, in which the wires are disconnected at one end one at a time and a battery and galvanometer connected to each line in succession at the other end, the test man at the latter end noting any advance upon the ordinary deflections, which will indicate excessive leakage.

Contacts will also be indicated by this test, and by the dropping of the indicators if in contact with exchange wires.

Breaks are indicated when the test men at the two ends are unable to speak to each other on the lines, and also by putting a current to line through a galvanometer, the other ends being all joined to earth. Partial breaks are shown by less deflections than usual being obtained.

The faults on the lines are located as far as possible by testing to intermediate stations, if there are such, and then handed to the linesmen concerned.

The lines should be periodically tested with more sensitive instruments for insulation, resistance, conductivity, and capacity, records being made of the results for future comparison.

CHAPTER XIV.

UNDERGROUND WORK.

ONLY a very small proportion of the telephone lines of this country are at present run underground, but it appears likely that there will be a great extension of their use in the near future, and that we shall have to follow the lead of the United States, where underground lines are becoming very general. A short description of the methods followed in America should therefore be useful.

The principal objection made to underground lines is the increased cost of installation, but it appears certain that the diminished cost of maintenence of a good system would soon counterbalance this. A more serious objection is in regard to the increased statical capacity, which seriously affects long-distance working. The main point, therefore, in regard to the design of cables for the work is to ensure that the capacity of the wires is kept as low as possible.

On account of the great number of different forms of cable used in America, a conference of leading experts met in New York in 1889 to arrange for a uniform type of cable to be used for underground work. The decisions arrived at were as follows :

The cables should be composed of 50 double wires. The wires to be 1˙025 mm. (= 41 mils) diameter of copper, the conductivity to be not less than 98 per cent. of pure copper. Each wire should be covered with a double coating of braided cotton. The wires should be laid up in layers ; in cables of 50 double wires, the centre layer to be of three double wires, the next of 9, the next of 16, and the outside layer of 23 double wires. Each layer to be laid up in an opposite direction to the preceding one.

The cable thus formed should be placed in a pipe made of 97 per cent. lead and 3 per cent. tin. (This alloy was adopted in order to preserve the pipe from the injurious action of creosote.) The vacant space in the pipe should then be filled with some insulating compound. The inductive capacity of each wire, after laying down, should not exceed 0˙18 microfarad per mile,* and the insulation resistance should not be less than 100 megohms per mile. The pipes should be protected by a coating of asphalte, with an external covering of two layers of fibrous material impregnated with some preservative compound, and laid on in opposite directions.

Several cables have been made by different firms conforming to these suggestions, but differing in details.

---

* These suggestions have been modified by a later conference. The maximum capacity is now ˙09 m.f. per mile. Artificially dried cotton, or specially prepared paper, is used for the insulation of the wires until each is a dia. of ⅛ in. The containing tube is ⅛ in. thick and 2 ins. dia.

The Paterson "Conference" Cable, made by the Western Electric Company, is the one which is most extensively used in America. The insulating compound used inside the pipe is melted paraffin impregnated with carbolic acid, and made into a froth with dry air. This is forced under pressure into the pipe and penetrates the cotton covering. The mixture has a very low specific inductive capacity, so that the capacity of the cable is reduced to 0˙16 microfarads per mile. The insulation resistance is about 100 megohms.

The " Faraday " Conference Cable is made by the Faraday Electric Company. The insulation substance is pyroligneous oil forced into the tubes. The outside of the latter is protected with jute impregnated with asphalte.

The price of the above cables runs about 3s. per foot.

Cables are now being introduced in America in which specially-prepared paper forms the insulating medium between the wires, resulting, it is said, in the reduction of the capacity of a conference cable to, in some cases, 0˙08 mf. per mile, with very good insulation. Such a cable ought to have a promising future.

Other cables are used for underground work, which do not differ materially from the cables used in this country for general telephone work, as described in Chapter XI.

Conduits.—Receptacles for the cables, called *conduits,* are constructed under the roadways, generally close to the curbstones, and are of several types. Three types, given on next page, appear to have turned out most successful in America.

1. *Creosoted Wooden Blocks* are laid in cement, some 3 or 4 ft. under the roadway, having holes about 3 or 4 in. dia. for the reception of the cables.   Such conduits appear to have stood the test of experience very well, the only trouble with them having been an injurious action of the creosote on the lead tubes.   The alloy of lead and tin recommended by the Conference completely withstands the action.

2. *Cement-lined Pipes.*—These are constructed as follows :—A sheet-iron tube, 8 ft. long, is held vertically. Inside this is placed a smaller brass tube, and semi-liquid cement is then poured into the space between the tubes.   When the cement has solidified the brass tube is withdrawn, and the tube, with others, is then fixed underground in a bed of cement, the tubes being connected in lengths by means of a kind of ball and socket joint.   *Ducts*, as they are called, formed of these tubes appear to be rapidly increasing.

3. *Wrought-iron Pipes.*—This appears to be the most successful form of duct.   The pipes are 20 ft. long and ·217 in. thick.   In laying them, a trench is dug about 4 ft. deep along the side of the street.   A layer of hydraulic cement concrete is then laid and rammed on the bottom.   On this is laid a row of iron pipes, side by side.   On top of these another layer of concrete, then another set of pipes, and so on until there are sufficient ducts, a thick cover of concrete being laid over all. The pipes are joined end to end by a coupling screw-joint, so that they can be quickly put together.   The inside of the tubes is often asphalted to prevent rust.

S

Manholes.—In order to place the cables in the ducts, and to make the necessary connections to them, *man-holes* are provided along the route. Along the principal conduits these are generally constructed of brickwork,

Fig. 215.

well cemented to render them water-tight. They are made about 6 ft. square and from 5 to 10 ft. in depth, at distances of about 70 yards apart. Fig. 215 is a section of a manhole, showing the iron casting which is placed over the brickwork, reaching to the level of the roadway. To this are fitted two round or oval covers, one large and heavy at the street level, and the other, a smaller one, below, the latter being made to fit closely by india-rubber on to the ledge of the casting, so as to render the manhole perfectly water-tight.

Ventilation.—The great trouble with the underground system is not with water, but coal-gas, which leaks from the mains and finds its way into the conduits and manholes, forming, with the air, a dangerous explosive mixture. Many serious explosions have occurred by the gas becoming ignited in some manner. To prevent the accumulation it has been found necessary to ventilate the subways by means of fans placed at convenient points and communicating by special pipes with several manholes. A hand-fan for temporary ventilation is shown in Fig. 215, which also shows the iron cage used over the openings to prevent accidents.

Drawing in the Cables.—To enable the cables to be drawn into the ducts what is called *rodding* is resorted to, and consists in passing a flexible steel rod of about ¼ in. dia. through from one manhole to the next, or, which is considered a better plan, a set of wooden rods provided with joints so that they may be put together to form one long rod is threaded through. When the next manhole is reached a rope is attached and drawn back by the aid of the rods, unjointing the latter as they come out.

The cable or cables, sometimes to the number of six, are then firmly and carefully attached to the rope and are drawn into the pipes by the men alone, or more often by the aid of a winch or windlass. All rough or sharp edges about the pipes must be carefully avoided to prevent damage.

Jointing of the wires and cables requires great care and considerable skill. Unless carefully done it will give rise to much trouble. To cover the joints made in connecting lead-covered cables, a lead tube is used about 18 in. long, and large enough to slip on the cable-tube. This is slipped on one cable before the jointing is done. When the latter is completed the wires are tied together, the lead sleeve is drawn over them and soldered on to the pipes by a plumber's *wiped* joint, the sleeve having been previously filled with paraffin wax.

Distribution of the Wires.—From a manhole near the premises to which the wires are to be joined, small subsidiary ducts are laid to the wall of the nearest building. Cables are threaded through these and other pipes to the roof of the building, where a pole is erected, from which open wires are radiated to the subscribers' premises. The distribution constitutes the most difficult part of the arrangement.

Many thousand miles of such ducts are now laid in America, New York city alone having considerably over a thousand miles.

CHAPTER XV.

MISCELLANEOUS TELEPHONE APPARATUS AND APPLICATIONS.

Automatic Call-Office Arrangements.—In most towns having a telephonic exchange public call-offices are provided, into which any person may enter, and, by paying certain charges, be put into communication with a person at some other office connected to the system.

In many of these offices a special apparatus is provided which serves to collect the money and at the same time automatically call up the central office.

Many different forms have been invented, but probably the first one operated by coins was that of Messrs. Crossley, Harrison and Emmott, which was originally constructed with the view of being used in connection with an ordinary subscriber's instrument, to enable him to pay a certain amount each time he used his instrument, thus paying on the *toll* system, instead of, or in addition to, a yearly subscription.

A box was provided with a slot large enough to admit

a penny. When the latter coin was put through the slot, it rolled down an inclined tube and fell on to a balanced scale pan, which overbalanced and allowed the coins to fall into a cash drawer underneath. At the same time a contact was closed in a local circuit which included an electro-magnet. The armature of the latter being attracted pressed against a contact, completing the line circuit to the telephone set. Being polarised, the armature remained in that position until, at the end of the conversation, the operator at the central office sent a current through the line and the electro-magnet, by means of which the armature was attracted to the other side and the telephone set again disconnected from the line circuit.

Mann's Automatic.—The next apparatus of the kind was invented by Mr. J. J. Mann, and was designed to automatically cut off the user after the lapse of a certain period allowed for conversation, in addition to signalling the office and checking the money paid. It was arranged somewhat the same as the automatic sweet-boxes, with the addition of a clock, which caused a disc to revolve once during the time allowed for conversation. The writer is not aware of its having been brought into practical use.

Poole and McIver's Automatic.—Figs. 216 and 217 represent an instrument designed by the writer, who believes it was the first put into practical use. It was arranged to serve the same purposes as the " Mann " (and was invented about the same time), with the addition of showing which of two charges (a trunk line charge of 6d., or a local charge of 3d.) had been paid. It was also arranged that the time allowed for a conversation should commence from the time the subscriber asked for was in communication with the caller.

Fig. 217 shows the inside mechanism :—A A'are the tops of the shoots, into which the coins are dropped through slots in the lid of the box, as shown in Fig. 216. C C' are the scale pans on to which the money is guided so as always to fall flat in the same position. When 3d. in coppers has been placed on C, it overcomes the counterweight D, and pulls down *e* until the coppers fall through holes into the cash drawer below. When D tilts up, a rod, E, attached to it leaves the spring F, against which it normally presses, and

Fig. 216.

allows the latter to make contact with a battery contact, G ; F being included in the line circuit, a current is sent through the line wire to the central office. The right-hand scale operates in a similar manner when sixpence in silver is dropped on to it, but a current of opposite polarity is sent from another battery contact.

Fig. 218 shows the apparatus required at the central office to distinguish the calls. The line from the call-office is first connected to the ringing key *k*, the back contact of which is connected to the polarised relay Re (shown with cover removed), the armature of which is polarised by a permanent horseshoe magnet. The relay is provided with two contact stops, to which are connected the two drops shown. The armature is connected to a local battery, and when deflected to one

Fig. 217.

stop causes the drop marked 6 to fall; and when deflected to the other stop by a current of opposite polarity, the indicator marked 3 is dropped.

The operator, seeing one of the indicators fall, answers by pressing the battery key *k*, and connecting her instrument to the call-office line. The current sent to line passes through the electro-magnet G, Fig. 217. To the armature of this is attached a rod, H, which, when the armature is attracted, raises the pawl of a ratchet wheel, J, for a certain distance, at the same time moving an index finger, I (shown also in Fig. 216), to the position marked O. The pawl in its normal position presses a spring,

L, in the line circuit from contact with a pin connected to the telephone set fixed in conjunction with the box. The wheel J is kept continuously revolving by the clockwork shown, and gradually carries back the pawl until it again presses against the spring L, which it does at the end of three minutes, the time allowed for conversation. When the operator has got the subscriber asked for, she again operates the electro-magnet G, and sets the index finger at *o*, thus ensuring a full three minutes for conversation.

Fig. 218.

Trouble frequently arose through the fact that a subscriber asked for could not sometimes be got, and that no means were available for returning the money, To obviate this a special press-button was attached to the instrument.

Instead of putting in the money in the firs

instance, the button was pressed and sent both a positive and negative current to the central office, causing *both* the 3d. and 6d. drops to fall. When the subscriber asked for was obtained, the operator instructed the caller to put the money in the slots, and checked the receipt by observing the indicators and listening to the coins being dropped in the box.

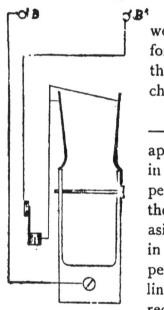

Fig. 219.

The above apparatus has worked well in many Lancashire towns for some six years, about thirty of them having been in use in Manchester alone.

Smith and Sinclair's Apparatus. — This is simply a checking apparatus, signalling being done in the ordinary manner. When pennies are put in the slot provided, they fall down a shoot and press aside two small springs, as seen in Fig. 219, which interrupt a permanent current put on the line by the operator. The latter receives a signal on a bell or galvanometer for each coin put in.

When a sixpence is put in another slot, two other springs are pressed aside for a moment and break the primary circuit of the induction coil. This break causes a sharp click in the listening operator's receiver. The boxes are also provided with slots, into which special keys, supplied to ordinary subscribers, can be inserted, and, on turning, give the necessary signals to the operator. In this way the subscribers may make free use of the call-offices.

The above apparatus is extensively used in the Glasgow district.

Cotterell's Apparatus.—This is the simplest checking arrangement of all. The coins, after running through the shoots, strike against bell-gongs. The gong for the pence has a different tone to that for the sixpence, so that the operator, listening whilst the coins are put in, can readily distinguish which gong has been struck. The instrument is much used in the Birmingham district.

Mix and Genest's Automatic Call-Box.—This is a checking apparatus which is substantially made, and would appear to answer its purpose very well. Fig. 220 shows the instrument open and with a telephone set attached.

When a coin of a certain value and size is inserted into the slot, it first passes through an arrangement which tests its diameter and thickness and rejects it if not satisfactory in those respects (directing it at once into a refunding box at the bottom). If satisfactory, it is guided into a grooved channel, where, after depressing a lever, which closes the line circuit, if its weight is satisfactory, it rests on the upper of three wheel segments, the rims of which protrude into the grooves. These segments are geared together, and are revolved by a lever connected to the armature of an electro-magnet. When the armature is attracted, the coin is

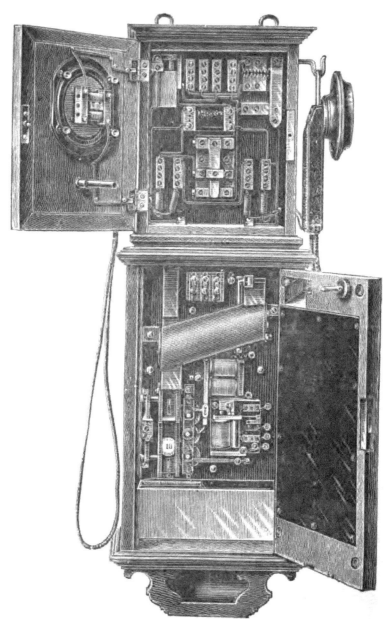

Fig. 220.—Scale $\frac{1}{6}$.

released by the turning of the segment and falls until arrested by the second segment, and on the release of the armature it falls to the third segment, where it rests until the ring-off signal is given, which operates the electro-magnet, turns the segments, and allows the coin to fall into the cash-box, pushing aside, on its way thither, a lever which breaks the line circuit to the telephone set.

If the line required is engaged, the electro-magnet is not operated, and the caller presses a white button, which turns the upper part of the grooved channel about an axis and releases the coin, which falls into the refunding box at the bottom of the instrument.

If the caller should neglect to ring off and the coin be left resting on the third segment in the groove, the coin inserted in the slot by the next caller presses aside a small roller attached to a lever, which operates the segments and releases the coin left in.

This and the other call-office instruments could be used in conjunction with a subscriber's instrument to enable him to pay each time he uses his instrument, on what is called the toll system. This system would appear to be the most natural way of paying for the use of a telephonic exchange instrument, only that it ordinarily entails so much extra clerical labour, which an automatic apparatus, such as above described, would dispense with.

Theatre Arrangements.—Much interest was evinced at the Paris Electrical Exhibition of 1881 in the arrangements by which the operas performed in the

Théâtre Français were transmitted to a room in the exhibition, and there listened to with delight by thousands
of visitors.   Fig. 221 shows the manner in which the
apparatus was arranged.

Ten Ader transmitters, T, *t, t, t, t,* and T', *t', t', t', t,*
were fixed five on each side of the prompter's box.   Each
transmitter was connected by a double line to eight
Ader receivers fixed in the room at the exhibition.

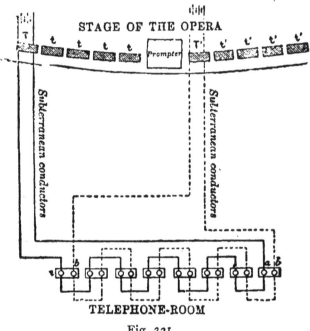

Fig. 221.

These, with eight other receivers connected to a transmitter fixed on the opposite side of the prompter's box,
formed eight pairs for eight listeners.   Fig. 221 shows
the connection of two such transmitters, T and T', to

sixteen receivers arranged in pairs, *a b, a b.* A listener using a pair of receivers would thus be connected by the left-hand one *a* to the left-hand transmitter T, and by the *b* receiver to the right-hand transmitter, T'. With such an arrangement the transmitted sounds will be most intense from that one of the two transmitters which is nearest the singer on the stage, so that a distinctly different effect is obtained from the two receivers of each pair. The effect of a singer crossing the stage is very curious and realistic, being somewhat analogous to the action of a stereoscope in giving solidity to a double photographic picture. In the case of the telephone it is difficult to imagine that the singer is not close in front of the listener.

The arrangements adopted in Manchester for transmitting operatic music from the theatres has for many years given great pleasure to those who have been privileged to listen. Two Marr transmitters are used at each theatre, suspended by india-rubber bands to the sides of the proscenium, at about six feet above the stage-floor, and arranged to point towards the centre of the stage.

The battery of four gravity cells for working each of the transmitters, instead of being provided at the theatre itself, as at Paris, is placed at the central office, the induction coils for working being also fixed there. By such an arrangement the current can be switched on and off at any time without going near the theatres.

Fig. 222 shows the manner of connecting up so as to be able to connect the secondary wire of the induction coil to any subscriber's line wire :—A represents one of the theatre transmitters, one terminal of which is earthed and the other connected to the line to central office, where it is joined to the primary wire of the induction coil B (res. about 1 ohm). The other end of the primary wire is connected to spring-jack C, to which a battery may be connected by the plug and cord D.

The ends of the secondary coil of B (res. about 50 ohms) are connected to jacks G and H. Through G one end gets earth, and by H a single wire line may be

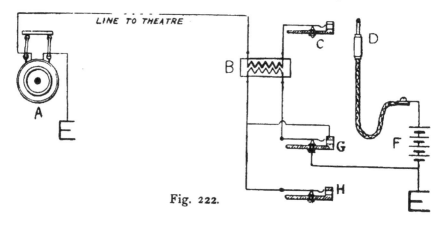

Fig. 222.

connected by a plug and cord, or a metallic circuit line may be connected and the earth cut off by plugging a double plug and cord into G.

A frame is provided on which is connected twenty or more receivers, which may be joined up in various ways, such as all in one circuit, or so that alternate receivers are joined up to transmitters on opposite sides of the stage, as in the Paris installation. Thirty or forty receivers may be worked by one transmitter with very little weakening of the sounds.

The writer has, with the above arrangement, provided many musical evenings to his friends, who have invariably expressed their delight at the results.

Police and Fire Alarms.—The use of the telephone for the purpose of joining up branch fire and police stations to the chief offices is becoming pretty general, and has proved its utility on many occasions. In America much greater use of it is made for such purposes. Alarm boxes, containing ringing apparatus and a telephone set, are fixed in prominent positions in the streets. The chief citizens are provided with keys for opening these on any occasions requiring aid. To prevent illegitimate use, the keys to the boxes are numbered, and it is arranged that after being used to open a box, they cannot be withdrawn from the lock until a policeman arrives on the scene and releases them.

Communication with Divers.—The helmets of divers are now provided with transmitters and receivers, to which are connected insulated wires connecting to a telephone set in the attendant boat, so that continuous communication may be kept up between the diver and the men at the surface.

T

APPENDIX.

The Collier Receiver.—This instrument has lately excited considerable interest in telephonic circles, and is based on rather novel features.

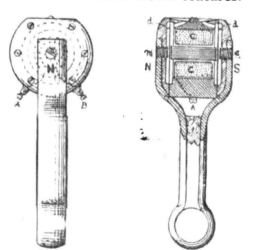

Fig. 223.—Scale ⅛.   Fig. 224.—Scale ⅛.   Fig. 225.—Scale ⅛.

A section of one form of the instrument is shown in Fig. 224, a side view in Fig. 223, and an end view in Fig. 225. A bobbin of wire, C, C, with a soft iron wire core is fitted into a round ebonite block. On each side of the bobbin soft iron diaphragms, *d* and *d'*, are clasped round their edges by outside covers of ebonite. A magnet, N S, has its poles let into the covers, and through both magnet and covers are screwed the soft iron pieces *n* and *s*, until they nearly touch the diaphragms. The top of the instrument is shaped for fitting to the ear, and is put into communication with the internal spaces between the diaphragms and the sides of the bobbin by small holes, as shown. The ends of the coils are connected to terminals A and B.

The diaphragm and coil are in a strong magnetic field, the core of the coil being strongly magnetised by induction.

It is claimed that the instrument is much more powerful than other receivers when used for long distances. Mr. W. E. Heys has made experiments showing that the Collier receiver gives an audible sound (from a ticking metronome) through a resistance of 4 megohms, whilst with other receivers of the best form the same sound was inaudible after 0·4 megohms had been included in the circuit. To some extent this result may be accounted for by the fact that a large number of turns of wire are put on the coil of the instrument, the resistance of which is about 300 ohms.

Mercadier's Bitelephone.—From his researches on the theory of the telephone, M. Mercadier has formulated the relations (mentioned on page 63) which should exist between the different parts in order to give the most powerful effects with any size of instrument. By following up these results he has constructed single receivers weighing less than 1¾ ozs. (ordinary receivers weigh about 14 ozs.), which are as powerful as those of ordinary size, and give in many cases clearer articulation. The bitelephone shown in Fig. 226, with attachments, weighs only 4¼ ounces, and is so designed that it may be kept pressed to both ears without the aid of the hands. The two receivers T and T are connected by the steel wire V V, which may be bent to give any desirable pressure on the ears. T and T

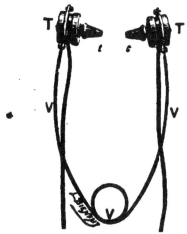

Fig. 226.

are furnished with ear-pieces, *t* and *t*, which enter into the ears, and sustain the instrument, which is used in the manner shown in Fig. 227. The ear-pieces *t* and *t* are covered with tubes of india-rubber, as shown, which assist the instrument fitting into the ears, and exclude external sounds. These can be changed, so that the objection of the same ones being used for different persons may thus be overcome.

The instrument would be specially useful for the operators in switch-rooms, on account of its lightness, and of its allowing both hands to be free for making connections.

It is obvious that the bitelephone will be extremely

Fig. 227.

convenient in any case where it is desirable to leave both hands at liberty for writing, etc., whilst receiving or transmitting a telephone message.

ABSTRACT OF PAPER

ON THE

TELEPHONING OF GREAT CITIES.

By A. R. Bennett, M.I.E.E.

Read at the British Association Meeting, 1891.

The paper discusses how the extensive demand for
telephonic exchange communication, which, in the
course of a few more years, is certain to arise in all
large cities—a demand of which no conception can
be formed from the present condition of telephone
exchanges in this country—can be met and satisfied.
Given low rates and a fairly-efficient service, the time
will come, and that at no distant day, when every
shopkeeper, and almost every householder, will look
upon a telephone exchange connection as as much of
a necessity as gas or water.

Indications are not wanting, even now, of what may
be expected when the inhabitants of large towns come
to realise what an important business and social
auxiliary a properly conducted telephone exchange is ;
for in Galashiels, and some other towns, there is already
a telephone for every 200 inhabitants, the principal
supporters, after the manufacturers and merchants,
being professional men, shopkeepers, and householders.
If telephoned to the same extent as the towns named,

London, with its 5,600,000 inhabitants, would possess 28,000 subscribers ; but owing to its greater wealth and extent, it is not only possible, but almost certain, that eventually London will require a telephone for ever 50 inhabitants, which, with its present population, would mean 112,000 subscribers. That number would only represent four times the proportion already existing in the small towns referred to.

A successful telephonic scheme for London, or any large town, would require to comprise several essential conditions. Firstly, privacy and efficient speaking must be secured ; secondly, the connecting together of subscribers and their subsequent disconnection and, if required, reconnection with others, must be rendered rapid and certain ; thirdly, the rates must be within the reach of small shopkeepers and householders, and should not exceed £8 per annum ; fourthly, the system must be laid out so as to be capable of indefinite expansion, without the necessity of periodical reconstruction ; and lastly, the undertakers of the system must have equal rights with gas and water companies in laying their conductors underground. All these requirements, excepting the fourth, have from time to time severally been met and conquered, but no existing exchange system, so far, comprises them all, although, technically and commercially, it is perfectly practicable to combine them so as to attain as nearly to perfection as possible. The sanction of the Legislature to the laying of underground conductors constitutes the only doubtful quantity.

The Post Office has demonstrated the feasibility of perfect privacy and effective speech in conjunction with a system of underground wires ; and the Mutual Telephone Company, in their recently-constructed Exchange at Manchester, has shown that privacy, distinct speech, and rapid and certain switching are quite compatible with as low a rate of subscription as £5 per annum. The only essential requirement that has not yet been demonstrated, is the laying out of a system so as to permit of vast and easy expansion in every direction ; and this, the paper shows, is a problem admitting of easy solution, provided that the laying of wires is made independent of private caprice.

The leading feature of a cheap, efficient, and easily-extensible exchange in a large town is a division, as far as feasible, of the area to be telephoned into sections not exceeding a square mile in extent, with some smaller ones in situations where, as in the City of London, very great commercial activity prevails. In the centre of each section will be situated a switch-room, to which the wires of the subscribers resident within that square mile will be led. As some subscribers will be resident quite near the switch-room, and others at maximum distance from it, it is assumed that, with the mile squares, the average length of a subscriber's line will be about a quarter of a mile, and, therefore, cheap to construct. Each of these secondary switch-rooms will be connected, according to the geographical configuration of the town, to either one or two central switch-rooms by a sufficient number of junction wires.

Such a multiplication of switch-rooms would be impracticable with the ordinary methods of switching, but a system exists which has been thoroughly proved in practice during the last nine years, and which is specially applicable where a very large number of subscribers has to be dealt with. By the aid of this system, which is known as the "Mann," or a modification of it devised by the author, with the switch-rooms distributed as described, the maximum time for establishing a connection between two subscribers situated at the extreme opposite limits of a telephone area as large as London would not exceed ten seconds.

The "Mann" switching system only requires apparatus at the switch-rooms of extreme simplicity and compactness, and calls for only a minimum expenditure of labour on the operators, while it interposes no obstacle in the shape of signalling electro-magnets at the intermediate switch-rooms to the freest possible passage of telephonic speech. The system is, consequently, better adapted than any other for communicating over long distances.

Privacy and long-distance speaking would be secured by the universal adoption of metallic circuits. Such a system would afford the maximum possible telephonic efficiency, and would enable (supposing it were likewise fitted in other towns) London subscribers to talk from their own offices direct to the offices of subscribers, not only in the most distant cities of Great Britain and Ireland, but in Paris and other continental cities. It is asserted that such a system would lead to such a rapid and phenomenal increase in the number of subscribers, that an annual subscription of £8 would, even in the largest towns, be sufficient to yield a large profit on its cost. even if all the wires were placed underground.

NOTE.—In a letter published in the *Times* of August 29th, 1891, the Duke of Marlborough states that: "A New Company . . . is about to promote a Bill before Parliament next Session with the object of establishing a complete twin-wire telephone service for the whole of London, on the basis of a £10 a-year rental, and with a system based on the plan worked out by Mr. Bennett, so that the telephone will be available to everybody for their business, their shopping, and their social needs."

BRITISH STANDARD WIRE GAUGE.

S.W.G	Nearest B.W.G.	Dia. in Mils. 1 Mil= ·001 in.	Pure Copper Wire at 59° F.			Weight in lbs. per mile. sp. gr. 8·9
			Resistance.			
			Ohms per yard.	Ohms per Mile.	Yards per Ohm.	
4	4	232	·000575	1·01	1740	862
5	5	212	·000687	1·21	1458	719
6	6	192	·000838	1·48	1194	588
7	7	176	·000997	1·75	1004	497
8	8	160	·001208	2·13	815	408
9	9	144	·001941	2·63	671	331
10	10	128	·001885	3·32	531	262
11	11	116	·002296	4·04	436	215
12	12	104	·00286	5·03	350	176
13	13	92	·00364	6·41	275	135·8
14	14	80	·00483	8·50	207	102·4
15	15	72	·00595	10·47	168	83·0
16	16	64	·00754	13·26	133	65·7
17	17	56	·00988	17·39	101	50·1
18	18	48	·01345	23·68	74·5	36·7
19	19	40	·0193	35·2	51·8	24·7
20	20	36	·0238	41·8	42·1	20·4
21	21	32	·0302	53·2	33·2	16·35
22	22	28	·0394	69·4	25·4	12·54
23	23	24	·0537	94·5	18·65	9·20
24	24	22	·0638	112·4	15·67	7·75
25	25	20	·0773	136·0	12·95	6·40
26	26	18	·0952	167·5	10·51	5·21
27	27	16·4	·1144	201·2	8·75	4·33
28	28	14·8	·1409	248·0	7·10	3·51
29	29	13·6	·1675	294·5	5·975	2·95
30	30	12·4	·201	354·4	4·98	2·45
31	—	11·6	·229	404·5	4·37	2·15
32	—	10·8	·265	467·0	3·78	1·86
33	31	10	·309	544·8	3·24	1·60
34	32	9·2	·364	642·0	2·75	1·355
35	33	8·4	·438	770·5	2·28	1·129
36	34	7·6	·535	942	1·87	·924
37	—	6·8	·668	1175	1·49	·740
38	—	6	·863	1519	1·16	·573
39	—	5·2	1·141	2010	·878	·433
40	35	4·8	1·340	2360	·747	·369
41	—	4·4	1·595	2805	·628	·311
42	36	4	1·929	3412	·519	·255

INDEX.

WILLIAM RIDER AND SON, PRINTERS, LONDON.

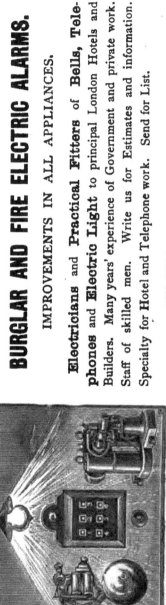

Square Crown 8vo cloth, 2s. 6d. to 5s. per vol.

THE object of the projectors of this 'Library' is
to provide a series of easy introductions to the
Physical Sciences, suitable for general use. Each
Volume will be well illustrated, and will embody
the results of recent scientific investigations.

ASTRONOMY. By G. F. CHAMBERS, F.R.A.S. With
134 illustrations. 4s.

LIGHT. By SIR H. TRUEMAN WOOD. With 85 Illustrations. 2s. 6d.

CHEMISTRY. By T. BOLAS, F.C.S., F.I.C. [*In the
press.*

GEOLOGY. By A. J. JUKES-BROWNE, F.G.S. [*In the
press.*

THE PLANT WORLD. By G. MASSEE. With 56
Illustrations. 3s. 6d.

MINERALOGY. By DR. F. H. HATCH. [*In the
press.*

ELECTRICITY and MAGNETISM. By S. BOTTONE.

ANIMAL PHYSIOLOGY. By W. SNODGRASS, M.D.

LONDON:
WHITTAKER & CO., 2, WHITE HART ST., PATERNOSTER SQUARE.

WHITTAKER'S PRACTICAL HANDBOOKS.

FULL LISTS FREE UPON APPLICATION.

The Practical Telephone Handbook and Guide to Telephonic Exchange. By J. POOLE (Wh. Sc. 1875), Chief Electrician to the late Lancashire and Cheshire Telephonic Exchange Company, Manchester. 227 Illustrations. 3s. 6d.

The First Book of Electricity and Magnetism. By W. PERREN MAYCOCK, M. Inst. E.E. With 85 Illustrations. Cloth 2s. 6d.

The Optics of Photography and Photographic Lenses. By J. TRAILL TAYLOR, Editor of the *British Journal of Photography*. *Immediately.*

The Art and Craft of Cabinet Making. By D. DENNING.
In the Press.

The Electro-Platers' Handbook. By G. E. BONNEY, 208 pages. 62 Illustrations, and full index, 3s.

Metal Turning. By a FOREMAN PATTERN MAKER. With 81 Illustrations, and index, 4s.

Practical Ironfounding. By the Author of *Pattern Making, Lockwood's Dictionary of Mechanical Engineering Terms, etc.* 212 pages. 109 Illustrations, and Index, 4s.

Electro-Motors: How Made and How Used. By S. R. BOTTONE. 166 pages. 64 Illustrations, and index. Second Edition Revised, 3s.

Electrical Instrument Making. By S. R. BOTTONE. Fourth Edition Revised. 202 pages. 65 Illustrations, and index, 3s.

Electric Bells. By S. R. BOTTONE. 204 pages. 99 Illustrations. Third Edition Revised, 3s.

Electric Light Installations and the Management of Accumulators. By SIR DAVID SALOMONS, Bart. With 438 pages and 106 Illustrations. Sixth Edition Revised. 6s.
"Contains a vast amount of really useful information."—*Electrical Review.*
"From a practical point of view the work is an excellent book of reference."—*Electrician.*

Electric Influence Machine. By J. GRAY, B.Sc. 252 pages and 89 Illustrations. 4s. 6d.

Electricity in Our Homes and Workshops. By SYDNEY F. WALKER, M.I.E.E., M.I.M.E., Assoc. M. Inst. C.E. Second Edition. With 320 pages and 127 Illustrations. 5s.

Foden's Mechanical Tables. Fifth Edition. Cloth 1s. 6d.

Wood Carving. By C. G. LELAND. With 86 Illustrations. Many of them full page. Foolscap 4to. 170 pages. 5s.
"A splendid help for Amateurs and those beginning the trade. Without exception it is the best book I have read at present."—Mr. T. J. PERREN, *Society of Arts Medalist, Instructor in Wood Carving at the People's Palace.*
"I consider it the best manual I have seen."—Miss HODGSON, *Instructor in Wood Carving at Manchester Technical School.*

Drawing and Designing. By C. G. LELAND. 1s. Sewed. 1s. 6d. Cloth.
"Full of valuable practical suggestions for beginners."—*Scotsman.*
"The book deserves the widest success."—*Scottish Leader.*

WHITTAKER & Co., PATERNOSTER SQUARE, LONDON, E.C

www.ingramcontent.com/pod-product-compliance
Lightning Source LLC
LaVergne TN
LVHW011941060326
832903LV00045B/127